# YOU MAY
# PLOW HERE

# YOU MAY PLOW HERE

*The Narrative of Sara Brooks*

Edited by THORDIS SIMONSEN

*Foreword by Robert Coles*

W · W · NORTON & COMPANY

NEW YORK · LONDON

FRONTISPIECE PHOTOGRAPH: *Sara Brooks, 1976.*

*The text of this book is composed in Palatino, with display type set in Palatino. Composition and manufacturing by the Maple Vail Book Manufacturing Group. Book design by Marjorie J. Flock.*

FIRST EDITION

Library of Congress Cataloging in Publication Data
Brooks, Sara, 1911–
    You may plow here.

    1. Brooks, Sara, 1911–        2. Afro-Americans—
Alabama—Biography.    3. Farm life—Alabama—History—
20th century.    4. Alabama—Biography.    5. Alabama—
Rural conditions—Case studies.    6. Afro-Americans—
Alabama—Social life and customs.    I. Simonsen,
Thordis.    II. Title.
E185.97.B82A35    1986    976.1'00496073    85-11534

ISBN 0-393-02257-9

W. W. Norton & Company, Inc., 500 Fifth Avenue, New York, N.Y. 10110
W. W. Norton & Company Ltd., 37 Great Russell Street, London WC1B 3NU

1 2 3 4 5 6 7 8 9 0

*You can't beat nobody down so low till you can
rob 'em of they will.*

—Zora Neale Hurston
*Their Eyes Were Watching God*

# Contents

# Foreword

A S I READ this compelling autobiographical narrative, an addition of inestimable value to the tradition of carefully edited oral history, I kept thinking of a woman my wife and I knew when we lived in
Georgia during those critically important years of the civil
rights struggles in the early 1960s. This woman was sixty
and had been born in a small town in South Carolina. As
a black child she watched her parents move off the side-
walk upon the approach of white people—a gesture of
submission. The image never left the child's head, and as
a woman edging close to her social security years she
recalled that spectacle and felt the urge to speak, if not
deliver a sermon: "Oh Lord, I will close my eyes and see
my momma and my daddy walking, and then the white
folks coming, and then my momma would pull on me and
on my two brothers, and she'd call to daddy, and we'd
step aside for them. Afterward we'd be back on the side-
walk, and my momma would be telling us we shouldn't
even come into town, because back there, where they
worked the land, no one would bother them. She'd always
say this, momma would to us: 'You children grow up to
fear the Lord, and love Him with all your heart, and you
children grow up to work your burden—and then every-

thing will be alright in the end.' I can still hear her speaking that message to us—and I've been telling it to my own kids, and to my grandchildren now that I have them."

She was a proud person—determined and stoically knowing. Her personal dignity was obvious, even to the casual observer. She had a way with words and phrases—such as "work your burden," a literary inheritance she drew on and gave to her sons and daughters and to the twelve grandchildren she would later have before she "passed to His world," as her husband referred to her death. She may have remembered her own and her people's humiliation, moments upon moments of them, but she also had every good reason to remember all the strong and resilient aspects of her social and cultural heritage. When we refuse to acknowledge this terribly significant side of their lives—the enduring courage of rather hard-pressed country folk, later become city residents—we do her, and individuals like Sara Brooks, no justice at all.

I need not speak for Sara Brooks or her wonderfully tactful, sensitive, and caring listener and admirer, Thordis Simonsen. This book is the last one to require yet another smug or patronizing interpretative summary from one of our all too abundant and authoritative social scientists. Let me, as a matter of fact, simply say that I wish such people, our various secular experts, would have the time and inclination to sit down with this book and read it for enjoyment, above all, but for other reasons as well: to learn, to be put in awe, to be made curious. So many questions rightfully come to mind as one goes through this book. What are the sources, for example, of such a person's eloquent assertiveness, her ongoing self-reliance, her knack of survival? Our novelists, needless to say, know better than to try to account for such virtues in people like Sara Brooks—know that the categorical formulations and generalizations of psychology or sociology are no match for the thickly textured rendering of human experience that a storyteller naturally offers us with no embarrassment in the face of life's ironies, paradoxes, inconsistencies, and, yes, mysteries.

All through Sara Brooks's life skeptical observers might have pronounced her prospects slim, her odds for survival poor. Still, she kept up her particular struggle, did so with energy and resourcefulness and even a touch of flair. The day will come, one hopes and prays, when this nation's history will include mention and acknowledgment of such people in our books and memorial statements; when a Sara Brooks will be as honored at White House dinners and awards ceremonies as any politician or military general; when a grateful nation will bow respectfully in eager tribute to the longstanding and exceptional contribution individuals such as Sara Brooks have kept making, year after year, since the founding of the Republic, to our national life, to our economy and our culture both.

Robert Coles

*Harvard University*
*March 11, 1985*

# Preface

WHEN she was thirty-seven and I was four years old, in 1948, Sara Brooks began to work one day a week in my parents' Cleveland household. Over the years I enjoyed her friendship and regarded her as family, but I knew so little about her—only that she wished to return South to visit her family, and that she sang hymns while she worked. Yet my personal interest in her caused me to turn an appreciative ear when, in 1974, she began to recount her rural childhood experience.

Sara Brooks is the product of the storytelling tradition, and she was born a performer. I asked her to engage an audience through a taped interview—a far cry from bantering with friends and relations gathered on porches or by firesides—and she did so artfully. She reconstructed situations in detail, she varied her syntax, and she incorporated many sensory impressions and much dialogue into her account.

Our meetings occurred rarely over the course of a decade. Once or twice a year I traveled from my home in Denver to Cleveland, where Sara Brooks resides. We met at my parents' house or at hers for several hours on each of several days running. During our first taping session in June 1974 she spoke almost without interruption for an

hour. I wrote an extensive agenda for each session there-
after, but my first prepared question was often my last,
because one memory generated another in a sequence dis-
tinctly personal, meaningful, and unpredictable. Although
in due course she willingly returned to detail accounts,
had I not whenever possible deferred to her own instincts,
I would have documented the facts, but not the fabric of
her life.

From the beginning I understood that Sara Brooks's
narrative account would enlarge upon, not duplicate,
existing literature on the twentieth-century black experience. Theodore Rosengarten's *All God's Dangers* and Jane
Maguire's *On Shares* document the life of a man, a tenant
farmer, a lifelong resident of the South. But this book records the life of a woman, the daughter of a freeholder, a
migrant North. Even in broad terms, Sara Brooks's story
has never been written.

Sara Brooks redrew her rural experience from an urban
perspective. Even though she associated urban comforts
with heaven, she defined her childhood life on the farm
in utopian terms. She understood that the rural life she
had known has passed, but she used the memory of the
farm as a touchstone in her quest for meaning and fulfill-
ment.

Sara Brooks reexperienced her country life with an
immediacy that stirred my own sensibility. When the exu-
berance of her unencumbered childhood years gave way
to the pain of her difficult transition years, my role changed.
She was no longer communicating through me to a larger,
remote audience. She was addressing herself only to me.
She voiced her humiliation as well as her pride, her dis-

grace as well as her dignity. Moved and honored by the trust she had vested in me, I offered back my esteem.

Sara Brooks's spirit, honesty, and insight compelled me to interact with her. It remained to prepare the portrait of her life that would command the attention of others as she had commanded mine. I transcribed approximately fifty hours of taped interviews and cross-indexed the approximately seven hundred pages of typed transcript containing her life story.

Editing followed. To preserve the distinctiveness of Sara Brooks's voice, I rendered her speech verbatim, except when her meaning might be unclear. The reader will find varied forms of the same word (for example "because" and "cause," "would" and " 'd", colloquial usages (for example, "that" to mean "so that" and "what" to mean "that"), and lack of agreement in verb tenses and personal pronouns. When appropriate, however, I made some changes for clarity: for example, when "of" was pronounced "a" I wrote "of," and when "and" was pronounced "an" I wrote "and."

With regard to content, again I rendered her account as faithfully as possible. But I did remove distracting digressions, combine multiple versions of the same story, and cut meaningless repetition. I retained repetition when Sara Brooks employed it for emphasis: Will Brooks provided for his family; the children did not philander, but they worked; and Sara Brooks enjoyed fishing and home cooking! While I adhered to her style of reminiscing and preserved as many natural transitions as possible, I did impose an order on material gathered intermittently over a ten-year period.

Although I crafted her autobiography, *You May Plow Here* is the narrative of Sara Brooks. "All these things I've *done*. It's not something that I *heard*. These things I'm telling you, I have done *myself*."

THORDIS SIMONSEN

*Denver, Colorado*
*1985*

# Acknowledgments

WITH unlimited gratitude I delight in acknowledging Sara Brooks for her enduring patience and trust; Helen Yeager for her sensitive literary counsel and gentle encouragement; Howard Klein for his generous donation of computer time; Beth Bethel for her invaluable academic counsel; Amanda and William Madar for their warm and lively hospitality; Kathleen Anderson for her confidence in the manuscript.

# Introduction

*You may plow here*
*Just as much as you please.*
*You may plow here*
*Just as deep as your knees.*
*But I will tell you*
*Right before your face,*
*You ain't goin make nothin here*
*But burrs and weeds,*
*But burrs and weeds.*

EACH SPRING when time came to break up the land for planting, Will Brooks harnessed his team, plowed, scratched through it, plowed on till sundown. And with every addition to his brood—another child born or relation taken in—he opened up new land for planting. Often he worked alone in the company of birds, and his lyric interpretations of their songs sometimes proclaimed a cropper's plight.

But Will Brooks never wavered; he planted, cultivated, and harvested a crop. And when his crop was made, he clapped his hands and worked on. He began farming in this spirit in 1905 when he made ten bales of cotton on fifty-three acres of rented land on the outskirts of a small

ON THE OPPOSITE PAGE: *Will and Hannah Brooks, 1975.*

town in west-central Alabama. By 1917 he had earned title
to the farm, and until he was whipped by the wrath of a
hurricane in 1940, he continued to plow his homeland.

Sara Brooks, his daughter, was born in 1911. In her
first year, her mother died a tragic death, but her grandmother Brooks and later her stepmother Hannah Brooks
adopted her. They loved her as their own, but Will Brooks
was his daughter's provider and keeper.

Supporting a family in Alabama's Black Belt in the early
1900s challenged a farmer: tirelessly he coaxed an exhausted
land to produce. But landowners like Will Brooks fared
better than their tenant neighbors, because the farmer who
owned his land also owned his crop. He conducted his
business with the white bankers and merchants directly,
as required, and as a free agent. He was free to sell his crop
for cash at favorable market prices, and he could then pay
up his debts for supplies purchased on credit during the
preceding growing season and thereby avoid high interest
rates charged on accounts due. If money remained, he could
buy household goods and farm supplies at lower cash
prices.

Tenure also permitted Will Brooks and other members
of the owner class to administer their land. White land-
lords forced tenants to plant cotton almost exclusively, but
wise landowners elected to raise table foods and fodder as
well. Food self-sufficiency protected the family against
hunger or debt in years when the boll weevil or weather
ruined the crop. And it allowed the landowner to invest a
portion of his cotton money in commercial fertilizers, which
improved productivity and boosted the family income.

Will Brooks raised food crops in abundance. He put
out ample fertilizer, and he managed his cash adeptly—he

never fell into debt. Consequently, his daughter enjoyed the security of a settled existence on the family homestead.

Although Will Brooks worked without pause to sustain a host of dependents, he relied on each, in time, to contribute to the farm enterprise. Sara Brooks was prone to mischief rather than discipline, play rather than labor, but her father's persevering nature tempered her persistently devilish spirit. She learned responsibility at an early age, and participation in farming became a fact of life, not a punishment.

Because he successfully bore the weight of his farm and family, Will Brooks won the respect of his black neighbors—tenants and freeholders alike. He served as the head deacon of their church, and they turned to him in times of need. Sara Brooks thrived on the community fellowship, and her father taught her to return the respect he had earned.

Tenure elevated Will Brooks's standing within his black community and eased his relationship with the local white community. Land ownership, however, did not exempt him or his family from segregation and discrimination sanctioned by Jim Crow legislation and practiced widely throughout the South. To minimize their influence, he and his family ventured beyond their black community only when necessary. As a result, Sara Brooks never witnessed overt conflict between blacks and whites, and she never learned to judge people on the basis of color. She went to church, she went to school, and occasionally she went to town, but she was always home before sundown.

Although her father urged her to continue her schooling, she had no way to estimate the potential value of education. She left school after the tenth grade. What she did learn of a practical nature was farming. And given her time, her location, and her family experience, a knowledge of farming ought to have sufficed.

In 1930, when she was nineteen, Sara Brooks married a farmer. She labored in the fields and bore children just as her mother had done before her. But her husband inflicted his rage upon her, and her escape from him carried her far afield.

Like most emigrants from the country, she left home with scant belongings. She was forced to give up her first three children because, without employment training, she could not hope to support them. Instead, their grandparents raised them in the fields.

Sara Brooks agonized over the separation from her husband's children. She also suffered the moral and economic burden of two additional children, born outside of marriage after she fled her husband. Each time she relocated—first to a town ninety miles from the farm, then to Mobile, and finally to Cleveland—her brother or a stepsister provided room and board until she could manage independently. Neighbors who understood her continuing hardship volunteered child care while she worked every day.

With the exception of early, intermittent factory jobs, Sara Brooks worked in domestic service. By the time she reached Cleveland, she drew higher wages, saved, and in 1957 was able to fulfill the vision of home ownership that had carried her through the turbulent transition years. In the meantime, one by one, her dispossessed sons moved to Cleveland to be with her. The restoration of her family was her ultimate solace.

Sara Brooks undertook life in the city prepared solely with the values her father had instilled in her—honesty, work, respect for others, and faith in God. *You May Plow Here* attests to her spirit for life, and especially to the hope and determination she set against hardship.

# YOU MAY
# PLOW HERE

# ONE

◇──◇──◇──◇──◇──◇──◇──◇

# We Had Some Farm

W
HEN we come home from school, we'd pull off our dresses—our gingham dresses what we'd wear to school each day—and we would put on our work dresses and go into the tater bank and get us some raw sweet potatoes. Then we'd go by the well, draw some water, and rinse em off and dry em off and put em in our pocket and get goin. We'd go in the woods and we'd get lightwood. Do you know what lightwood is? It's a wood from a pine tree that has dried up, and it makes real good kindlin. We'd take the axe and we'd take a croker sack, which is a burlap sack, and we'd go and we'd cut this lightwood off the stumps and put it in the sack, and we'd bring it to the house for kindlin the fire. We'd eat supper later on after we'd get through with our work, so we'd take with us a knife and these sweet potatoes from the bank, and we'd go and sit down in the woods in a little low place where the wind wouldn't whistle. And we'd peel our potatoes and just eat these raw sweet potatoes.

Oh, I used to love to eat raw potatoes! Crunch, crunch, crunch. Sweet potatoes! We grew sweet potatoes—red and white sweet potatoes—and Irish potatoes and cabbage and collards and turnip greens. We grew all that in the garden. Momma had a garden right by the well where she just had her strawberries, she grew garlic and onions, and what else she had in there? Butter beans—they are always raised around the palins cause they grew on the palins. We call it palins which is boards fence—and mustard, beets, radishes, and string beans and English peas. Oh, and we had tomatoes in the garden. Shooks, we'd have rows tomatoes long as from here I don't know where—about seven or eight long rows of tomatoes. They'd be layin down everywhere—red, just pretty red ripe tomatoes. And we had peach trees and purple plums in the garden. We had Elberta peach trees in the garden, and the seeds fall under the tree and they would come up and my mother would set out little ones. They'll grow.

And we'd raise our own cantaloupes and watermelons—long rows of watermelon out in the fields—and a few hills of squash by the garden, and rows of okrie at the back of the house. And we had fields around the house that we had peas—black-eye peas and speckled peas—and sweet corn. And then, too, some cotton was raised around the house. Oh, they was big fields, wasn't they! Big! They was big, the fields around the house!

But we had fields away from the house that was bigger than that where we raised peanuts and corn and millet, ribbon cane and some cotton. All these was raised away from the house. You could look for just I don't know how far, and it'd be so pretty with the cotton be so level all the way across, and then it goes to the cornfields, and then the cornfield is high all the way across. It was beautiful—it really was—and we had a lot. Everything that we ate mostly we raised it ourselves, except our sugar and our flour. We had some farm!

We raised our own chickens and our own hogs—sometime be twelve, fifteen of them hogs runnin around. And we had cows—we had a lotta cows which we milked every day. Then we had turkeys we'd kill at Christmas time, and guineas we had—guineas always was around the house. The guineas be "pot-rack, pot-rack, pot-rack." You ever heard a guinea say that? The guineas be sayin somethin like that. And the old turkey be "gobble, gobble," and the roosters be "coo *coo* coo *coo.*" We always had plenty to eat, and it was busy, you know. Somethin's always goin on on the farm.

And the first house that we lived in was a *two-roomed* house. It had one chimney, and that one chimney made two fireplaces, one in each room. No one lived there then but my father, my brother, and my grandmother and me. My father and Davey slept in one room, and my grandmother and me slept in the other room—in the same bed—I slept in the same bed with my grandmother.

We slept in the same room and cooked in the same room. We cooked in either one of the rooms, but my grandmother mostly cooked in her room—on the hearth in her bedroom. You could cook biscuits or cornbread. Get the coals from the fire and make a little pile of coals on the hearth and make the bread and put it in the spider—they had legs to em high enough to let the fire not be smothered—and put a lid on the spider and set the spider over the coals. Then you put some coals on top of the lid, and that would brown the bread both bottom and top.

And my grandmother would cook vegetables on the hearth. She had this black pot with legs, so she would put vegetables in this pot and set it on the fire and cook vegetables. And if we had boiled meat, she'd boil meat there. We didn't know anything about makin *beef* roast or anything like that cause everything was boiled cause we didn't have no stove. So we used to cook on the hearth—my grandmother used to cook there.

I thought that my grandmother was my mother. I don't even remember when my mother died because when my mother died, I was only nine months old. So my grandmother's the only mother I knew, and I didn't know that she wasn't my *mother* until my father's fixin to marry. I was six years old, cause he married when I was goin on seven. So Davey told me we's fixin to get a "new momma," and I say, "What about new momma?" Say, "I ain't gonna have no new momma cause Grandma is my momma." I didn't know no better. And he said, "Grandma ain't our momma," says, "our mother's dead." But I didn't believe, so I went to her and asked her and she said, "No," she wasn't our momma. So, when my father married, well, we did have this new momma. I was six years old.

So my grandmother raised me from nine months old until I was six when my father married, and then I was raised by my father and my stepmother which was a *very*, very sweet lady. My father only by that time had three children, but one of them had died. There was me—I'm the baby—and the oldest one, because the middle one had died with meningitis. So when my father married we had this good stepmother, and she raised me and my brother. Then she had nine children of her own, but we all seem as whole sisters and brothers because they loved us, and they gave us all that they were able to give us. It was a lot of us—my father provided for all of us—and he did it evenly, you know what I mean? Just because I was another wife's daughter, he didn't make no difference. He loved us all—it was evenly. Likewise with my stepmother—she didn't seem to love her children better than she did me. And so it was love in our home.

We all worked hard—we all worked hard and we got what we could—and my father took care of all the family. He took care of his grandmother until she died. Then he took care of his mother until she passed. Then he took his sister's children and raised them right along with me. It was two of them, Rhoda and Molly. Then he took care of his crippled brother, which was named Jim, until he passed. My father did all this.

He worked every day and we had our little house, and from time to time he had more built onto this two-roomed house. When he got married he had an addition put on this house which was the kitchen and a dining room. And when my father had this kitchen built, then he bought a stove, an iron stove with a reservoir to it. And when the family began to expand and was gettin bigger, my daddy kept addin more to it till we had a kitchen, a dining room, and a company room—for the company if the company came. We keeped that company room closed every day until Sunday—and three bedrooms and a porch on this house. That's where we was raised up.

We lived in the country and we wasn't livin really close around anyone, so we'd love to get out—we'd get out and go to church in order to go someplace. We'd go to Sunday school and we'd stay to church. Our church didn't have a meeting but once a month, so we'd stay at our church those Sundays, and if our church didn't have a meeting that Sunday, we'd leave our Sunday school and go to another church. We'd go to Trimble first Sunday, second Sunday we'd go to Horizon, third Sunday we'd go to Pleasantville, and the fourth Sunday we'd go to the Methodist church.

See? That's the way we went. But we went *every* Sunday cause if we didn't, we'd just be back over in the woods and nowhere to go. So we'd get up and go to Sunday school every Sunday; then we'd go round to church.

So we went. Some Sundays we walked. That was a *long* walk, so we started early and we'd walk. And sometime somebody passin in a wagon would pick us up and we'd go. But when we walked we went barefeeted, and we'd go through the woods and across little branches walkin logs. Sometime we'd stop and play in them—you know how kids do—and when we'd get to church, our feet be wet because we went in the water. But we taken us in a bag a wet towel, and when we get near the church we'd wipe our feet—all the dust off our feet and legs—and put on our shoes and our stockins and go on to church. Our shoes be shinin when we get there! Goin back, when we got to a certain distance, we'd pull em off and go on home.

My father was a deacon in the church—the head deacon—and he was dutiful about goin to church. He would lead hymns in the church, and he'd pray in the church, and every third Saturday he would go to deacon meetings. He'd work in the mornin and then he'd come home and take his bath in the tin tub—you know that's what we had, tin tub. And my mother always kept his clothes fixed—he'd wear a pair of clean overalls and a clean shirt. He didn't dress up—only dress up on Sunday—but he would be clean. He'd go to the deacons' meeting, and then when he come home in the evening, well, he didn't do nothin else that day but maybe sit around the porch and study his Bible.

And when he come home from church on Sunday, after he'd eat dinner he'd be sittin down and we'd be sittin down and doin nothin, and things would be gettin dull—look like we wouldn't go nowhere. And he would be readin the Bible, and then he'll look up and he'll tell us different things—he used to tell us a lotta things about the Bible— and he'll go back to readin. And we be sittin around weepin over the next day counta gotta go to school or either gotta go to work.

# TWO

## *Laziness'll Kill You*

I N THE MORNINGS, getting up, my father would call
Rhoda first. He'd say, "Rhoda, get up! Rhoda, get up!
It's time to get up!" And Rhoda say, "Yes, Sir, Uncle
Will." And that's when Rhoda'd get the rest of us up, cause
I'd hear it too because she and I and Molly slept together,
so we all waked up by the same time. But I'd make like I
was asleep—I wouldn't say *nothin*—I wouldn't—I wouldn't
say *nothin!* I would be the last one to get up if it's possible.
Rhoda get up, Molly get up, and then I get up. We stayed
in bed long as we could, but we had to be up before six
because if we were goin to field, we had to get up and
cook.

So we'd get up and you make up your bed and go wash
up and get ready to get in the kitchen. Some start cookin
breakfast, and some goin to the cow pen, so whoever's
gonna cook, cooked, and the other two would go to the
cow pen and milk the cows. We'd carry water in a pail and
a rag and just go off the back porch. You come right on
out to this little trail and you go right down to the pasture
which wasn't very far from the house, cause we had a cow
pen there where we'd milk the cows.

We'd milk the cows evening and morning. What we'd
do in the evening, we would shut up the cows and let the

calves out, and we'd have to round up those calves in the mornin in order that they suck a little bit first to get the milk to come down, and those calves would be bumpin up under their mothers. And then we'd get the calves off from the cow. Then we would wash the cows' bags. Then we'd milk. You strip that tit, just strip it down, and that milk come squirt, squirt, squirt, squirt. You know, you'se holdin the bucket with one hand and you strippin the tit with the other one. You had to hold the bucket; if you didn't hold it, the cow would always have a foot in the bucket. So you be holdin that bucket and you strip the tit, and when you don't get anything outa there, you get over to the next tit. And as you fill this bucket what you holdin, you pour the milk in a big bucket you have over there on the ground. But sometimes the cow kicked the bucket outa your hand and wasted the milk, and then we'd just go to the next cow because, I mean, we'd get scold for being careless, but sometimes you just can't help it. Maybe the cow might have a sore tit cause the calf might bite it while he suck it, and if you bother a sore tit the cow will kick you quick. So when the cow kick the bucket outa your hand, you had to go and get the next cow and start milkin it. But after we take all the milk, we let the calves in to the mothers and let them suck awhile. Then we would come from the cow pen, strain the milk, put the milk in the churn, wash out the strainer and things and hang them up in the kitchen. Then we's ready for breakfast.

For breakfast we'd usually cook biscuits, and we'd have butter and biscuits and syrup and milk. We didn't have meat because in the summertime the meat would be about out because it always would get tainted—it wouldn't be no good to eat. So we'd have breakfast in the dining room,

and then when we get through eating, we's all ready to go
to field.

We'd be goin to field sometime at good daybreak cause
we'd always go to field real *early* so we'd work a lots before
it gets too hot. You know what I mean? The sun would be
so hot you could see little devils twinkling out in front of
you. Little things—they just quiver. We called em "lazy
jacks." It was the heat.

So we'd take our hoe on our shoulder, and we'd have
on our straw hats, and we'd be choppin corn or choppin
cotton—that's what we'd be doin. Or we'd be hoein the
peanuts—we had to keep the grass cleaned out. And oh,
the rows would be so long! To be in the field hoein, it was
awful to look from one end of the row to the other after
the sun gets hot. In the mornin time or in the evenin when
you know it's gettin near time to go home, you never think
nothin about it. But when it was hot in the day and the
devils would be showing, the rows were *long*—they were
*so long!* I'm tellin you, I didn't like that!

But we never had no time off—we always worked up
until noon. And when we's workin in the field, we never
knew what time it would be because we didn't have but
one clock, and that clock was at the house. So we'd stand
the hoe up, and if the shadow of that hoe gets short, you
know it's gettin along near twelve o'clock. And when that
hoe is *standin* on its shadow, you know it's noontime.

So we'd go under a tree and sit down. We had a lotta
trees around cause whenever it rained, that's where we
went—under the trees and stood. And when we're workin
in our own field, my mother'd bring dinner to the field
and we'd eat under the trees. She'd bring one big bucket
of peas, and then in another bucket she'd have greens.

We's always gonna have those peas and greens—be cabbage greens or collard greens—she's gonna boil a pot every day. And we'd always have cornbread. Then sometime she'd bring milk she'd maybe churned before dinner, and we had meat—big old hunk of boiled meat. Some of the little ones would come, too, and help bring the dinner. And then to top it off we'd always have some sweet. We'd have syrup bread, or we'd have a big old apple pie or some kinda pie or another—berry pie or peach pie. It was real good; it would be *so* good.

And if we's around the house, we went home for dinner. We'd have boiled peas or butter beans and okrie and cornbread. Or we'd have maybe turnip greens—hog meat cooked in with the turnip greens—and sweet potatoes that we dug from the ground. And we'd have dessert. We always had plenty to eat, that's for sure. And we'd drink good old cool water outa the well—put some syrup in it and stir it up and drink it. It's cool—and drink it right along with our dinner.

But if we was off in the field, or when we worked at somebody else's field, we carried our dinner cause it was too far to walk back home and wouldn't be nobody there to bring it. So we'd have to take us somethin and we carried it in a bucket. We'd take it in the mornin and we'd eat it at dinnertime. What we'd carry would be somethin like cornbread, and we'd take buttermilk—we'd always carry our milk. And we'd take some kind of a meat in the bucket. Mostly that's what we'd have. We didn't have no vegetables for dinner that day—my mother would have vegetables when we come *home.* So we'd eat our dinner, and then when we get through eatin we just rest awhile, and then we go right back to work.

My father come around pretty often when we's workin
in the field. He always was watchin. Nothin that we did,
but if we had did somethin, he was gonna see it. And
when we'd be done got tired—we kinda not workin so
hard and we gettin around too slow—he would tell us all,
"Listen at that bird." The birds would be singing. "You
know what that bird sayin?" We'd say, "No." He'd say,
"That bird sayin, 'Laziness'll kill you,' so let's get goin."
You know, *let's get goin* mean *go to work.* He'd be tellin us
to get up and get goin cause we'd be talkin—we used to
talk a lot to each other, and we used to fuss in the field,
fight in the field. Rhoda never fought and I never fought.
I never did fight nobody—I'd always stay out of a fight.
And I never did like to argue—I never did like that. So I
would stay clear.

But when we worked in the field, it used to be so hot
my father would buy us hats to wear—straw hats with a
wide brim. He would buy us one hat a year. That's all we
really needed—you don't need but one hat a year. And
we'd fight and tear up each other's hat—do that to spite
each other. One day my sisters started a fight because I
was the oldest one and I would tell them things to do, you
know, and they didn't want to do what I wanted them to
do. So they would like to get me—they always loved to
get me started. And so my second sister, she told the others, "Come on, let's beat her. Come on, let's beat her."
They'se fixin to jump on me, but I wasn't afraid cause I
was gonna knock em down if I could. If I couldn't, I was
gonna take what came. But as they got ready to beat me,
my father walked up. See, he'd always be around check-
ing. If we started fuss or somethin he'd be right around
there listenin. And we knows better than to cuss or say

any kinda curse word or anything cause you never heard him curse either. So we couldn't say no bad words, but we would fight—we'd fight. And he sat around long enough to see where the troublemaker was, and that's the one he'd get. Lotta times it was me. So they all was gonna jump on me one day, but my father walked up in time and give them all a good whippin, and that excluded me. So I was sittin on top of the world just laughing with my feet hangin down and knowin I was in the wrong.

And one time my cousin Molly—about this hat proposition—we'd tear up each other's clothes, we'd tear up each other's hat. The one that couldn't fight the most, if he can get a chance to tear somebody's clothes or tear up your hat, well, he done win. I say if you and me was fighting, and if I couldn't fight as well as you, I'm gonna get you some way or another if I had to tear your hat or your clothes. That's the way we fight. So my cousin Molly was gonna fight because we got to sputin over somethin, and I told her I ain't goin to fight. And so to make me fight she grabbed my hat, and my hat was new. She grabbed my hat and tore it. I said, "Oh, you done tore up my hat!" And she said, "Oh, we can get more hats." And my father said, "Sure enough, you cannot!" We didn't know he was around. You know, he slipped up behind us and we didn't know it. We got some good little old switchin all right, but it didn't kill us. Oh, brother, uhn, uhn. Look like I thought I shoulda had a better break than my cousins because it was *my* father, *my* home, and all that. But I didn't. My father treated us all the same.

But we never was lazy cause we used to really work. We used to work like mens. Oh, fight sometime, fuss sometime, but worked on. Sometime we'd stay in the field until about five o'clock in the evenin. Then we'd come home, and we didn't have too much to do in the summer when we come home but just to feed the hogs and milk the cows. We fed the hogs pussley. It'd grow in the fields, you know, in the crops. It'd grow big and spread over the ground, and it'd be great big bunches of it. We'd take a sack with us to the field and we'd pull the pussley on our way home sometime, and then we wouldn't have to go out after we got home. We'd go in our fields and somebody else's, too, sometime—people be glad for you to done got it out of the field. So we'd pull it up and put it in croker sacks and get croker sacks stuffed fulla pussley and bring it and throw it in the hog pen for the hogs. Oh, they loved that—they'd eat it. It was real tender. So we'd pull that for the hogs—we'd do that every evenin in the summertime. And on Saturday evenin we'd pull it for Sunday so the hogs could have some for Sunday, too. We didn't pull it on Sunday.

Then when we come in from work, we'd wash up. My daddy had a shelf for the water bucket out there on the back porch, and then down underneath was another little shelf for the wash pan and the soap. We'd use bar soap—we didn't have no sweet soap. So we'd take the dipper—my father made this dipper from a long-handled gourd—and you dip some water and put it in the pan, just get the soap and wash our face and hands. And we had a towel hangin on a nail—we called it a towel but my mother would make them from old sheets or either osnaburg. You dry your face and hands on that towel. Everybody use the same towel.

So we'd step on the back porch and wash up on our

way in. Then we'd go eat. Then we'd wash the dishes and all and get through doin that. And if it was summertime we'd take some chairs out on the porch at night and we'd sing. It was my two cousins and the smaller kids what was comin up under us and my brother. Oh, boy! We used to have a good choir! Really! It really sound good! You could hear our voices *goin way out* at night. And then when we'd sing so, some peoples over farther from us would hear us and they'd sing. The woods between us and the streams between us—it'd be real pretty. It was a good time! Oh, we used to have a good time! You see, that's the only entertainment we *really* had. We didn't have—these times these kids are havin now, they think is good. It's nothin, just nothin, really. And we hear the frogs—they'd be "whoop-whoop, whoop-whoop" down there in the woods. It was so quiet and everything.

We sit around on the porch till almost time to go to bed. We'd go to bed about seven o'clock—seven, eight o'clock. And, you know, it's the funniest thing when we were kids and we didn't have no bathtub. So what we did, we'd wash in the wash pan when we get ready to go to bed. You really took that good bath on Saturday night in the tin tub, but all the rest of the time we'd wash up in the pan. We'd wash our face and hands and underarms and privates and wash our feet. We'd wash our feet last. We'd be in the bedroom before the fireplace in the wintertime, and we're on the porch in the summertime. We could wash on the porch cause wasn't any boys around cause my brother was away, and we didn't have no 'lectric lights, so it's dark at night—it's real dark in the country. And in the summertime it'd be hot, so we'd wash—it be refreshing.

We put soap on the towel and you wash. Then you wring it out in the water and dry yourself off. We didn't have no dry towel like we do now.

But lotta times we just washed our feet. You got to wash your feet regardless if you took a bath or what because if we went anywhere, on our way back we pulled off our shoes. So we'd wash our feet—*had* to when you go to bed. The one what went and got the water in the basin, he'd go first and pass it on. "I'm next." "I'm next." You'd wash yours, and then you'd wash yours, and you'd wash your feet. That's the way we'd go round. Everybody'd wash your feet all usin the same water—me and Rhoda and Molly. And we'd take a towel and dry em off.

Oh, brother! I'm tellin you, you just don't know! I know these things—these are things I *know*, not what somebody *said*. But we always went to bed early—we was early to bed. As my father say, "Early to bed, early to rise, makes a man healthy, wealthy, and wise. Plow deep while slug-gards sleep, and you'll have corn to sell and corn to keep." So we had to go in early and get up early.

# THREE

<hr>

# *The Things He Knew How to Do,*
# *He Did Em*

**M**Y FATHER would get up early in the mornin, and after he ate his breakfast, he might have one strap fastened on his overalls, and one maybe be hangin down cause we laughed at him so many times—he'd be in a hurry and he'd be gone! He would go off to work like that *early* in the mornin. Sometime he would say he didn't want no breakfast and just get his snuff and go, and then he'd be in the field when we'd get there. See, he'd go first unlessen he's gonna drive the wagon. If he's gonna drive the wagon, everybody had to be ready when he got ready. You see, he probably wanna take his plow-stocks and other things because Rhoda would plow, and he would plow. He wouldn't drag the plow all the way to field hitched onto the mule—he would put it in the wagon, hitch the mules to the wagon. When he get there, he take the plow off and go to work.

So he'd plow all day and dip that snuff. And he never seemed as if he was tired—that's one thing he never did. I don't know why, but my father never did seem as if he was tired. And oh, he has been a *good* man cause he always looked out for us. And sometime if there wasn't enough food on down in the year, he didn't want nothin. He'd say, "Well, I don't want nothin this mornin." That's in order that we'd have it. See what I mean? We didn't understand it like that *then*, but we've learned since that if anybody went, likely it would be him. He always wanted us to have, and we never had nothin fine, but we had.

Some mornings my father'd get up *real* early and make him up a big fire outside the palin fence—the yard had a palin fence around it—and he'd sharpen all his plows by putting em in the fire till they get hot. And he had some tongs with a long handle, and when that plow get red hot, then he'd reach in that fire and pull it out and he'd put it on the anvil—he had an anvil sittin out there. Then he would beat that plow with a great big sledgehammer and dip it in the water what he had in this old hooped barrel— after he done sharpen it, he'd dip it in the water to harden it. That's the way he'd sharpen his plow. *Bam* bam *bam* bam *bam*. He'd beat it. You could hear it. In the country, wide open country, it was quiet, you know, and you could hear so *far!* We could hear other peoples when they'd be sharpenin their plows, too, like we say, "Mr. Harrison sharpenin his plows this mornin," or Mr. Jackson or Mr. Strong.

Oh, he was busy—he was a busy man. He really was. The things he knew how to do, he did em. He did all his wagon makin—he'd make all the bodies for his wagons. And sometime he had to replace spokes in his wagon wheels. And I've seen him fix collars for his mules and sew straps on his saddle and fix his plowstock. He'd fix things—he used to keep things goin. He'd do what he could.

At night when everybody's in and everybody ate and

everybody sittin around, well, my father'd be done got this white oak—some long tall pieces of white oak. He'd shave em down into strips, and he'd bottom our chairs with that. And he used to make baskets, too—great huge cotton baskets outa that oak. He would do that in the wintertime cause he'd be makin em for the next year. He'd make em for the next year cause nothin else to do in the wintertime. So he'd make baskets, and we'd be in our room, and he'd be in the other room, and we'd be runnin to and fro—the kids—we'd be runnin to and fro.

And I know when I was smaller I remember he used to have a fish basket he made outa white oak. You make it so the fish can't come out when they get in. My father used to set his basket at night. He'd set it in the branch— it wasn't too far from our house—and he'd go the next mornin and pull that basket, and oh, he'd have some fish! Really! He'd have a *basket* of fish! And he bring em home and we clean em up, and boy, we'd have more fried fish! Oh, I wish those days would come back.

But he'd make baskets, do chair bottoms, make brooms—he used to make palmetto brooms. Do you ever know what palmetto is? Kinda got little sticky things on it? Well, my father used to go in the big swamp and he cut these leaves off, bring em home, and let em dry. He'd always cut em in the fall of the year and he let em season in the smokehouse. Then when they get dry, he would get an old hoe handle or he would take a piece of a limb off a tree, and then he would tack these leaves on, one on top of the other one, all the way round till he make a broom. It'd be a big broom, and that's what we used to sweep our floors with.

We only had bare floors cause we didn't have no rugs.

It's just boards, board floors. We scrubbed the floors often with a big old scrubbin mop. My daddy made it outa board. He had put holes in it, and then you take shucks from the corn and you wet the shucks, and then you twist em and you push em through those holes, and when you get it all filled—full of shucks—then you could take it, put a handle in it, and then you scrub with it. We would use sometimes sand and lye soap, put the scrubbin mop in that water and scrub the floors—me or Rhoda or Molly—and they'd be just as clean as they could be. But that's the way we would scrub our floors.

And so what else did my father do? He used to make axe handles and he used to make hoe handles out of white oak by shavin it, shavin it, shavin it until he get it the shape he want. And he made his own palins. What he would do, he would cut down small oak trees and that would be the posts he'd put in the ground. And this palin came from pine wood. He cut it in blocks as you want your palins so high, and then he would split these blocks, and then he would go with his chisel to what size he wanted em. Just like now peoples go up to the lumberyard, but all our posts and palins came through by his hand-makin.

So my father did all that. And he used to go muddyin for fish with a hoe and a gig. You make a board and you nail nails down through it—sharpen the nails and nail down through and put a handle on it. That's a gig. Then you take your hoe and your gig and you go to a branch where the water's almost dried up when it's real dry in the summer. You go to the deepest part of the branch, and there where most of the bigger fish, they'll be in that particular spot. You take your hoe and you get in the water and you start stirrin up the water until you make it real muddy.

When you make it real muddy, then the fishes'll go to jumpin up, and when they start jumpin up you take this gig—*slap,* just *slap* with the gig because it's got the sharp nails. You know, every time you slap at a fish, he'd stick on the gig. You'd pull it off and put it in the bag—you have a croker sack bag hangin on your shoulder—or sometime they'd have an old big tub or bucket where you can throw it on the bank. So you keep on like that until you get all the bigger fish you want. Then my father'd come out and he'd get in the bushes and he'd pull his wet pair of overalls off and put on a dry pair, and he pulled off his muddyin shoes and dry off and put his other pair on. So that's the way he used to catch fish. That was muddyin for fish with a gig and a hoe.

And he used to get his lantern and go in the woods at night and cut down a tree—he had observed this tree already seein bees flyin around it—and he would get bee honey. We call it "bee tree" because bees 'll be in it. They'd have a hollow in it and that hollow is where the bees would be done made the honey. So he had to cut the tree down, and then he'd make a smoke so the bees wouldn't bother him too bad. He'd have his match and he had lightwood to make a fire and rags to make the smoke. That smoke from the rags would run the bees away while he'd get the honey. And my father would put old screen over his head to keep from gettin his face stung. Then he would rob that bee tree—we'd call it "robbed it"—and bring that honey home. Sometime he'd get about a lard can full of the honeycomb with the honey in it, and when we get up the next mornin, oh, boy! We'd have a good time eatin honey and chewin that honeycomb. We'd eat biscuit and honey— hot biscuits and honey was *real good.* We'd eat that honey and we'd chew that honeycomb, and then we'd have us a chewing gum for all day long. And we'd chew sweet gum from the sweet gum tree. Very seldom we had store-bought gum, but if we got a piece of sweet gum, that'd last us a long time cause we'd always stick it somewhere and go back and get it. Now it's true!

But my father used to get bee honey, and he used to go possum huntin, too, at night. My father'd go huntin around where a lotta simmon trees would be because they always would go up the simmon tree because they love simmons and they eat simmons. But you don't catch possums in the summer cause in the summer that's breedin time for em and they have young ones, so they hunt possum in the wintertime. My father would catch that possum and they'd break that possum's neck—put a hoe across that neck and *pull* the tail. And there always was a fire going, so my mother'd pull out some coals and take that possum by the tail and roll that possum in them hot coals until it burn the hair off it, and then she'd take a knife and scrape that hair off the skin. Then she'd gut him, you know, and then when she get through guttin him, she'd cut off the feet, but she left the head on. Then she would wash him real good and put some salt on it, and that would be to preserve this possum until she's ready to cook it cause we didn't have no freezer or refrigerator neither. So she'd let it go over night soakin in the salt water. Then she would boil this possum, and when she get through boilin it she would roast this possum in the coals— hot coals—and she'd have boiled potatoes all around it, and the head would be sittin up there and the possum would be grinnin at you. That's what I couldn't stand—I didn't want no possum till the head was took off cause the possum would always be grinnin. But when she took the head off, that possum would be *so* good. Boy, I'd be so anxious to get home so we could eat up this good possum!

And my father used to kill rabbits, too. That's another thing we used to have in the evenin. That was a delicious dish! My father'd go huntin for rabbits in the fall, and sometime he'd come back with lotta rabbits in his sack. If they're young, you fry em. If they'se old, you par boil em. And sometime my father'd catch a squirrel and my mother'd make a squirrel pie. Oh, boy! That's good! Yup, we had that, too.

It wasn't fine, but we had food to eat. And we wasn't well off—you can *never* believe that! But we did come up with *some* things that some didn't come up with. On Sundays we always had a nice dinner. We never lived in a rented place—we had our own home. And we had horses and we had mules. I reckon it's because my father—well, a lot of people didn't work, just like they don't work now. But I bet *we* worked! We'd be workin, and peoples be downtown meetin the train. It's a little town, Orchard. Used to be a train come through, and people would be down there at the depot sittin around downtown. My father never let us go down there like that. We didn't go places, but we'd have plenty at home.

My father always wanted to have his own and he always told us, "Always work for what you get." Cause I remember somebody went and broke in my father's smokehouse once and stole a whole can of lard. He knew who it was, and he used to steal from us. But my father would say, "Well, that's all right. If they need it that bad, let em have it." So he'd say that and go on.

I don't remember my daddy ever mentioning nobody

else stealin nothin from us, but peoples would borrow from us—they'd borrow anything they didn't have that they needed. They even borrowed so much they was borrowin fire coals. You ever heard of that? We livin so far from town, if matches give out—you look in the box and see you don't have but two or three matches to make a fire? Well, we always used oak wood on the fire and oak coals'll stay hot a long time. So while we didn't have no matches, we'd dig a hole in the hearth and put a big coal in there and cover it over, and then in the morning you can take lightwood and hold it to this coal and blow till you get a blaze. So I know all about that, too! It's just like I said— this is what we did.

So they keep these coals wrapped up in the ashes, and if they should happen to go out and they didn't have any matches, they'd send over to borrow some fire. We used to borrow some fire every once in awhile, too. "Go over Mrs. Harrison, get a coal of fire." The Harrisons lived over cross the field. We'd borrow a fire coal and carry it in a cup, a salmon cup. We'd hold it in a rag so it didn't get too hot and bring it home. Isn't that funny? We run outa matches and the fire went out in the house. We'd borrow some fire coals every once in awhile.

Or if my mother ran out of something she would send us down to Aunt Georgia's for it. But we didn't go around borrowing like a lotta peoples did. Peoples run out and they borrow cause maybe they didn't have the money at that time and town was a long ways to go. But they'd always wanta borrow somethin—flour, meal, lard, bakin powder. Name it! And my mother was always a good-hearted person, so if she had, she'd lend. Salt. You know it give you bad luck to pay back salt if you borrow it—it's bad luck.

But it ain't too bad a luck to come and get it! Milk. We always had milk because we've had as many as four or five milk cows. Some cows go out, some be coming in. So we'd milk twice a day and we'd churn twice a day. We'd milk the cows in the morning, put that milk in the churn, it'll be churned this evenin. You gonna milk this evenin and put *that* in the churn, and it can be churned in the mornin. So long as it's not churned, it's sweet milk. We'd put this sweet milk into our churn, and then you put some buttermilk that you already have in the sweet milk to make it sour. We'd call it "turn"—it would clabber. Now in the winter the churn had to sit by the fireplace in order that the milk would clabber, but in the summertime we could leave the churn in the kitchen because it would be warm enough in the summer that it would clabber anywhere. *Then* you churn it, and that makes that sweet milk buttermilk which we'd drink at night for supper, and butter which we'd wash and put in a mold, and we had the butter for breakfast with hot biscuits and syrup. But you got to churn the milk to make the butter come.

My grandmother would go out on the porch and churn the milk because it would be hot in the summertime, and when she would get ready to churn, she would tell us to break a branch off the chinaberry tree and come fan the flies. So we'd get a branch off the chinaberry tree, or either we'd get a peach tree switch, and we'd stand up over the churn and we'd just fan the flies to keep the flies from botherin the churn. So my gramma would be churnin—boom de boom de boom de boom. And Mrs. Harrison would send Winifred over or either Aunt Georgia would send Lydia and Irene over for some milk. Everybody had their own cows, like Mrs. Harrison and them, but sometime the cows go dry so they used to send over and my grandmother used to give milk. She never sold it. Then if our cows go dry, I never remember my mother sending us to nobody's house to get no milk. But they'd come after the milk about the time we'd churn and they be standin at the gate—they be standin at the gate waitin. So my grandmother made a song she used to sing to the churn:

> Come, butter, come, come, come.
> The calves are bleating,
> The cows are lowing.
> Little boy standin at the gate
> Waitin for the butter,
> And the butter won't come, come, come.

She was just churning the milk and she'd be singing it. She made this song up because somebody always standin around, comin with a bucket to get milk. Sometimes somebody be there with a four-pound bucket which is a lard bucket, and then sometime it was a syrup bucket which we'd call a can bucket. So somebody's always waitin for the milk cause we always had a lotta cows. And my father had a lotta peoples to feed, but he was blessed—I think he was blessed to feed all of us.

# FOUR

◇◇◇◇◇◇◇◇◇◇◇

# *It's Cracklin Bread!*

SO WE LIVED on the farm, and on the farm was pretty good. We raised our *own* hogs, and my father would kill the hogs in the wintertime. He would dunk the hog in the head with his axe—the hog standin there lookin at you, and you take and knock him in the head with your axe. Lord, ain't that somethin! Then my father and them would cut these hogs up and they would smoke this meat in the smokehouse. The smokehouse was big, but this particular place where he smoked that meat in the smokehouse didn't have no floor, and right in the middle of this dirt floor there was a place where they would build a fire. They'd go and get some bark from an oak tree and some hickory bark and corn cobs, and that is what he smoked the meat with. He would smoke it until the grease dripped out and it gets real dried, and when it gets dried, it was cured. Then it hung there until we ate it up. In the country it was just fresh air, and you could smell this meat smokin so *far*. It just smelled good! And you could tell people cookin biscuits. Oh, good old smells! But when they get through smokin that meat, it was somethin good, wasn't it!

But before you smoke the meat you trim the fat off, and the fat would go for lard, and the skin that the lard came out of was cracklins. We'd cut the fat and the skins up in pieces and put em in a pot, a big black pot with three legs on it sittin on a brick. It'd be outside the palins. Then we'd make a fire to it—the woodpile was out there. And somebody would sit there with a cracklin stick—my father carved it from white oak—and they would stir it and it would cook and cook and cook until it turned brown. When it turned brown and go to the bottom, well, that's cracklins. You take it, then you pour the fat up in a lard can—my father used to have lard cans. Then we'd take these cracklins and my mother would put em in a sack and let em drip, drip, drip to get the rest of the other fat out of it. Then she'd take these cracklins and she'd put em in big old crocks and we had that for cracklin bread. We kept these crock pots in the kitchen on the table, and whenever we wanna make cracklin bread, you go and sift some cornmeal—we had our own meal—and we put salt in it and we put soda in it—salt and soda. And then you'd crumble up this cracklins in it—a lotta cracklins—and put some buttermilk in it and make up this bread and put it in the pan and put it in the stove and cook it. When it gets done you talkin about somethin good. It's cracklin bread! And if you wanta really eat somethin good, it's cracklin bread and syrup and buttermilk. Oh, I love it! We'd have that in the evenin—that was a meal right there. Or we ate these cracklins sometimes at meals with sweet potatoes. They're good—those cracklins be so crisp and so nice!

Then, too, for our syrup, we never had bought any syrup because we raised sugar cane, and around last of September we stripped the blades off the cane with sticks. Then we cut the top out of this cane, and then my father and them'll cut it down and put it in piles and load it on the wagon and haul it to the cane mill and lay it down beside the grinder. Somebody feeds it into this grinder—the grinder is pulled by two mules—and that makes the juice which is strained through a burlap sack and drained off into a barrel. Every time the barrel gets full you put the juice into the pan where it's cooked, and when it's cooked the syrup runs off into another barrel. When it was full they put a corn cob stopper in the hole at the head of the barrel and they put the barrel on the wagon and carry it home. When they get the syrup home my father would put it in the smokehouse.

My father'd save all the skimmins when they make syrup—everybody would save their own, you know—and after it's worked that'd be the Christmas shinny. It's whiskey, you know, but they call it "shinny." They'd put the skimmins into a barrel and they would keep it in the woods somewhere. They'd put a sack over it and tie it around the barrel, and they would go and watch it every so often to see whether it's workin. Then when it's workin they'd put up this still. Cause I remember one night my daddy was makin it in the house—he used to make it in the house in the fireplace—and he stayed up all night that night, and he had a jug about half full this shinny. So next morning he said, "Come here, Davey. I want to show you what I got last night." My father went to get the jug and it hit against the chimney and just went all over the floor. Davey say, "So, Pa, that what you done last night!" It come out just as clear—like water—but it'll make you drunk. Cause I remember once I stole some of it and I didn't take but a swallow or two of it and I was sick. I didn't know what's wrong—I was so sick. So maybe I took too much.

In the fall we'd take the corn and we'd put it in the corn crib, and each Saturday mornin we would go to the

crib and we'd shell corn. We used to have a corn sheller—
you put the ear down in it. But when the corn sheller gave
out, we just shelled it by hand. Shelling corn by hand, we
used a cob. Put the ear of corn in one hand and rub the
ear with the cob, and you could rub all the corn off. Only
shelling we done was for grits and cornmeal and to feed
the chickens. My mother would feed the chickens in the
morning and also at night. She'd go out and get four or
five ears she'd have in her apron—you know, they had
long aprons at that time. She'd always carry the ears in
her apron, and she'd shell the corn off the cob, and she'd
throw the corn around the yard. She'd "Chick, chick, chick,
chick," and they'll come running. Some of em would be
in the yard and some would be down in the woods. They'd
come running and they be crackling, and my father say
when the chicken crackles they're sayin, "I lay every day;
I lay every day."

But you shells the corn until you get a bag of corn big
as you want to take to the mill, and when you take it to
the mill you can tell the man, "I want cornmeal and I want
grits." Then you get a bag of grits and a bag of cornmeal.
They put the grits inside of the cornmeal in a smaller sack.
My father'd come home and it'd be layin cross the mule's
back. And when my father come home with that corn in
the summer the mule's sweatin, and that *meal* would be
hot with the mule, too! But it's your own cornmeal and
your own grits from your own field.

So we had everything, everything that we needed to
eat and to have around our house exceptin sugar and flour
and rice what we couldn't make. So my father'd go to town
on Saturdays and he'd buy up these things and bring em
home. He would just say, "Well, Hannah, I'm goin down-

town," and he would ask her, "Now what to get?" She would write him a little list and give it to him. Then he'd go out and he'd hitch up the mules and the wagon, and he'd go on downtown and he would buy whatever we needed. He bought a sack of sugar—we used white sugar—and he'd buy flour in a barrel. We used to keep it in the smokehouse, and then I used to be a regular visitor eatin sugar outa the bag. Oh, I used to eat sugar! And he used to buy big cans of lard—two and three cans of lard we'd keep in the smokehouse. You know, we made lard in the winter after we did hogs. When the lard ran out my father would buy it, and when we buy it that'll last till we make it again. He'd bring it back in the wagon, but not all the time that he taken the wagon down. Lotta times he just went on the mule, specially if he didn't have to bring back a bucket of lard. If he's gonna get a sack of flour, some sugar, or somethin like that, he'd put it in one of these burlap sacks—big ones—and it'd hang over the mule, and he'd be sittin on the mule.

My father used to trade with Mr. James Brantley. He'd take up things—what you mean by takin up is gettin things on credit—and he would pay for em when he got some money. Being a farmer, he didn't have no money to come in till the end of the year when he harvest his farm un-lessen sometime he had somethin to sell. He would sell cows to white peoples if they wanted them cause they would buy em and make beef out of em. We didn't sell em all the time cause we didn't have no ranch, but he'd sell one every once in awhile. Or hogs he'd sell—peoples would come to the farm and buy hogs cause he used to have a lotta hogs. And we'd sell chickens, but we'd take em to town for that. Momma would take em or we would take

em. She didn't go to town often, but if Momma went to
town with the chickens, she'd go in the wagon with my
father and she'd carry some chickens and some eggs and
sell em to buy material to make dresses and thread and
things like that. She didn't sell nothin else like no butter
cause we needed it. And she didn't sell things from the
garden. If any neighborhood peoples come by the house
and she had peas or greens or butter beans in the garden
or sweet potatoes, she'd give em some. And Mrs. Harrison used to come over and my mother'd give her some
strawberries, and we had a great big bunch of garlic, and
when somebody come by she used to tell em, "Help yourself."

But now in the wintertime my father was workin out
at a place called Pineland. He was cuttin logs and rollin
logs, and he didn't come home till on the weekends. He
got some money that way. And he used to dig wells for
people—he'd make some extra money by diggin and cleanin
out people's wells. And he used to work on the railroad—
now he did that most often than anything else. His boss-
man was named Mr. Callahan, and he would let him work
on the railroad rainy days to make some extra money. When
they needed an extra man, why, he would leave his field
and go to work. He'd be workin on the section layin cross-
ties. But other than that, he didn't have no sources for
makin money, so he'd take up things and he'd pay for em
at the end of the year.

So my father would go to town, but we never hardly
went. He didn't say why, but my father didn't allow us to
go. Cause I remember once he went down to take my sister to the doctor—Sally, the one's next to me. When she
was small—my mother used to shell peas, and Sally put a

pea in her ear. The ear kept worryin her and she kept cryin and, you know, frettin. Finally it got bad, so my father took her to the doctor, and I wanted to go—I was gonna sit in the bottom of the wagon and hold the baby. "No," he said, "you don't need to go. Stay at home." So he went in the wagon and he carried her to the doctor, and the doctor got this pea out of her ear and he gave him some kinda medicine that had to be diluted with linseed oil. He just took it and put it in his back pocket. Coming home, the lid of the bottle worked off and he got burned on his, you know. So when he got burned, oh, that done me all the good in the world cause I say, "You coulda carried me. If you hadda carried me, that wouldn'ta happened." But him being a man that don't stay in for anything, he wouldn't pay no attention to it, so he got sorer and sorer. Finally it got so sore he couldn't wear no pants, and he had to wear a gown. He wouldn't stop—he was tryin to keep things goin. Even when he had to wear something loose like a gown, he'd be tryin to show us things and tryin to tell us what to do and all. So we made us a song—we said, "Pa gotta great big sore on him, but he don't mind. That big burn, let's heal it." That's when we'd be teasin him because he had this big sore. We just laughed, and it done me all the good because I wanted to go downtown and he wouldn't let me.

So we didn't go to town all that much, but when we did go, we walked unless my father would carry us in the wagon. But when I was much smaller, we had a surrey with fringes around it, and it was two seats in the surrey. I remember that real well. I used to love to get in that surrey, and we'd be ridin, and I'd be lookin out, and these fringes be wavin. Oh, boy! I was so glad when we had this surrey cause that was somethin extra at that time. And then we had a buggy, and the buggy just had one seat, cause I remember when my father got married, I went to the wedding and I stood in the back of the buggy and held onto the seat. So my brother and I rode to the wedding in the buggy, but we didn't get to ride back cause I wanted to get in that buggy and ride back with them and they wouldn't let me. I reckon it's newly bride. I had to walk back home.

Oh, and we owned a car! I forgot that. Peoples around there didn't have no car, but we had it. I was about thirteen when my father got this car. It was a brand new 1925 T-model Ford. My father bought it from Jackson Motor Company in Madison. He'd go downtown, go to the mill, take and buy food, and go to church. That's all he'd use the car for. But my brother went around courtin girls, so he'd take his girl friends around in the car. My father gave that car to Davey when Davey married Rebecca and left home. But we had a car shed, and Sunday mornin I would bring the car out the shed and bring it and put it under the pine tree—we had a pine tree there around the house. But that's as far as I got because my brother was gonna sure not let us learn how to drive. He didn't want us to learn so he would be the only one that could drive the car.

But, anyway, we had a surrey first, and then we had a buggy, and next we got this car. Then we always had a wagon, and we had these mules. My father always had two mules or a horse and a mule, but it had to be two because my daddy had a two-mule wagon. Let me see, Old Mabel and Old Maude and Old Daisy I remember was the horses. And Old Lightnin and Old John, those was our mules. But when we was small, my father would take my brother and me down to the train station in the wagon, and he would stay there until the train came and put us on. We was goin to a little place called Madison. He'd send us on the train to visit Gramma Duval. See, I was born in Madison. When the time come for me to be born, my mother went to her mother's so her mother could wait on her, so that's why I was born in Madison—that's where her mother was livin. Madison is fifteen miles from Orchard.

When my mother died my grandmother Duval wanted us to stay with her, so my father promised her that he would let us come to see her, and every so often he'd send us. We'd stay maybe a week or two, me and my brother. He'd write a letter to tell them when he's gonna let us go, and he'd put us on a train. Then my uncle Aber—that's my mother's brother—he was workin on the trains and he would always meet us. He was walkin on top of the freight trains. I don't know why he was walkin em, but I've seen him up there and the wind be just blowing—you could see how the wind was blowing his clothes. I don't know how far he went—he went from one junction to another little junction. So he would meet us if he was off, and if he was workin when the train got there my uncle Ruf—we called him Ruf but his name was Rufus—now he would meet us and take us to our grandmother's house. Uncle Ruf had a car, but when we was real little, he didn't have no car then cause he carried us in his wagon. It wasn't that far—we could have walked—but he always had a one-horse wagon.

So somebody would meet us at the train station and take us to my grandmother's house. She was old and she was poor, too, just like everybody else, but she always was real good to me. And Stella—that's my mother's sis-

ter—she would always be jealous of me cause my grandmother would give me things. You see, she used to work
out for peoples cleanin house, I reckon, and maybe even
cooking, I don't know. But I know she worked out for white
peoples and they would give her things, and she'd always
save the things that these peoples gave her and she'd give
them to me. One time she give me a little old silver-gray
hat, short in the back and long in the front. Oh! I treasured
that hat. It was somethin I dearly loved!

I remember once when we were going to Madison my
father carried us to the station, and he went over to the
store, and my brother was the oldest and supposed to have
been lookin after me. We had been waitin awhile for the
train, and it look like the train was gonna never come to
me. I just wanted it to hurry up and come on! I thought
we done waited long enough! When that train come around
that bend with the whistle blowin, I got on the track and,
"*Oh,*" I say, "*here* come the train, you all! *Here* come the
train!" I was just shoutin and dancin out there in the middle of the track, and the peoples pulled me off. I'm tellin
you!

That was the first time that I ever rode the train goin to
and fro to my grandmother's house, and the longest ride
I'd ever had until I came to Cleveland. But when the train
come through, everybody'd be standin on the platform—
there was a platform—and the white peoples was up here
and the colored peoples would be here. Now they wasn't
supposed to mix at all. And if you was colored and you
had to go to the bathroom, you didn't have nowhere to go
if you didn't go in the woods before you got there, you
know. You couldn't go in their restroom at the depot. It
was a restroom there and we knew we wasn't allowed in

there cause no colored people went in there. None. If I hadda went in there, they woulda snatched me out.

But when the train come everybody gets on the train, and those that was white would get on back there, and colored peoples had to ride on the front coach. They had seats in there for everybody to sit, they had a toilet for everybody to use. But that was your coach and back here was the white peoples' coach. Now for me knowing exactly did it look any better or what, I don't know because I didn't go back there. I wasn't allowed back there. But if there wasn't enough room in our coach, then we'd be mixed up with the baggage cause you go in the baggage car and stand up.

But you be sittin by the window and the train be goin along, and one place the train would stop and no colored peoples get off at that stop. That was a place they called Foxfield. Foxfield was a little stop between Springfield and Madison, and it was a sign on a post, "Niggers, read and run." The letters was in red up there on a board. "Niggers, read and run." I guess a lotta poor white people were livin there and they didn't want no colored people around in that place where they were livin, see what I mean? My father knew about it, but he didn't say nothin. And at that time we was just so glad to get on the train. We didn't say nothin and we didn't question anything. Nope. We just went. But when we start thinkin, gettin older, then we'd ask each other, say, "Wonder why?"

◇◇◇◇◇◇◇◇◇◇◇

# FIVE

# We Did It on Saturday

**M**Y FATHER would go to town and we'd stay home on Saturday because we had a lot to do at home. If it was urgent enough that we had to work, we worked in the field, but most the time we'd be home washin or either ironin our clothes and sweepin the yard and gettin ready for Sunday cause we worked durin the week in the field, and if it wasn't time for the field, we went to school. So if we failed to get the washing done during the week, we'd have to do it on Saturday morning.

We had a well, but something went wrong with the well. Until my father cleaned it out, we used to have to wash at a spring. The spring was in callin distance, but you couldn't see it from the house because it was in a little wood head. We had a trail on down to the spring—go right by a sweet potato patch on one side, and that would be extending to the garden, and the well was by the garden. And then on the side of the privilege [privy] was a cotton field would have peas and corn in the missing places where the cotton didn't come up too well. The trail go by there, and then it come on by the cow pen, through the pasture, and get under a wire and come around across another field and right on down to the spring.

We'd go to the spring to get water. Before my father

married my mother, my grandmother used to go to the spring with me if Davey wasn't home. I was afraid to go alone because in this spring used to be a lot of crawfishes, and I was scared of crawfishes cause I always heard if a crawfish bites you, he'd hold you till it thunder. That's what they used to say. But when we go down to get water these crawfishes would be swimming all around, and then sometime a big snake would go off in the water. I would be so scared I'd watch for the snake, and if I didn't see the snake, I'd hurry up and get the water and get out.

So my grandmother and I would go down to the spring, and she would take three buckets and give me two little can buckets,and we'd get water. Coming back, she would set one big pail of water on top of her head and have a pail in each hand. She could bring it just as nice and level all the way home, and I don't know how she did it. I couldn't carry no water on my head—I bounces too much. But I notice another old lady—that was Mr. Jackson's mother—she used to go downtown and she used to carry a little basket to put whatever she bought in, and you could see Aunt Mae comin down the road with this basket on her head. She be just a-steppin and it'd be sittin up there just like that! But, anyway, Davey and I was small, so when we would go to the spring, we'd go under the wire and through the pasture and on out because it was nearer way. But my grandmother'd go around by the watermelon patch, which she didn't have to go under the wire, and come out in front of the cow pen and home. She'd sit down one pail and then take that one down off her head. She'd have pails of water! But we had to cook—we had to wash greens. Oh, I'd hate the time we's gonna cook greens and had to wash em. And had to wash dishes—not wash clothes then with it cause we's washin them at the spring, you know. But we had to cook and wash up our own selves, and we had to bring the drinkin water home. So we was regularly goin to spring with those buckets, especially when it was hot cause you'd want fresh water, fresh cool water from the spring to drink.

One time Stella was visitin my mother and my father, you know, before my mother died, and she went down to this spring to water the mule. Davey wanted to go, so Stella gets on the mule, and my daddy set Davey in front of Stella for her to hold him. When they got down to the spring and the mule put his head down to drink the water, Davey slid off into the spring. You know, when you ridin a mule and you got a little one, you usually sit him in front. That's where Davey was sittin, and he slid right down! And instead of her gettin my brother outa the spring, Stella hops offa the mule and she runs clear back to the house to tell my father Davey had fell in. She'da left him in the spring, but he was big enough to get out. And my father was on his way down to get him—he's goin as fast as he could to see about it—and he met my brother comin back. My daddy used to tell this story—I didn't see this.

So we used to wash at this spring, and our tubs was wooden tubs made out of barrels—my father used to cut a syrup barrel in half, and that'd be two tubs that we washed clothes in at the spring. They had hoops on em, and we kept water in em so they wouldn't get too dry and fall apart. We'd soak the clothes in these tubs with lye soap which my mother would make from oak ashes, and then we'd put them on a battling block which is a big block you saw when you be done cut down a big oak tree. It had to be oak—then it wouldn't burst. You'd set that up and that be your battling block. And we had the oak stick what you battle with—it was made wide at the end—or sometime we'd get an old wagon spoke, but most of the time it had to be oak because pine'll get in your clothes. So you soap the clothes real good, and then you squeeze em and you put em on the battling block. We'd battle the clothes and we'd turn em over and battle the clothes some more. You washin em when you battling em—battling, battling. Then you put em in a big black pot. This pot would sit on rocks, and we'd get pine sticks from round in the area where we was washin because it was in the woods, and we'd put them under this pot and boil em. That was sterilizin em.

When we washed the clothes we'd pour the suds off in the stream, and the stream would run right into the cow pasture, and the cows liked to drink the suds. So when the cows would come to drink these suds, why, I'd scald em—I used to scald every cow that came to drink. I used to be real terrible on that—I used to love to see em run. We'd always take a bucket with us down to where we'd wash because we'd have to dip water out of the spring and put it into the pot, and when that water be boilin hot, I'd get this water and dash it on em. They'd go up through the woods, their tails be just goin, and they'd be flyin like mad! My father never caught that one, but I had got one good whipping about scalding the hogs—I used to scald the hogs, and I used to put turpentine on the cats' tails to see them run. So after my father given me such good whipping and then talked to me about how I would like for it to be me, then I stopped, and I guess I went to gettin better. So I'm a professional on being good now. But I used to do these things. Oh, boy!

So we washed our clothes, and the heavier things like

overalls and old shirts, you throw em on a wire by the pasture if it wasn't where the cows could get a hold to em—cows'll chew em up! But we had to bring all the sheets and pillowcases and our underclothes to the house from the spring. We'd bring em in a tub with a handle on each side and hang em on a line that run from one corner of the house to the other corner. And when we washed the clothes, if a spot was in there and it could come out, we's gonna get that spot out cause my grandmother'd take it off the line—"Take it back and wash it over!"

On Saturday evenings my mother would iron. We didn't iron the sheets and things—we'd let em dry on the line and take em in, fold em up. But my mother would iron my daddy's shirts and we'd iron our clothes. In the summertime you could iron outside on the porch. We put the ironing board between two chairs—they be straight chairs. It would be a wood board and we have it padded with sheets and we'd just iron on that. We would use smoothin irons, and we used to have a coal bucket—we used to get coal and you put coal in there. On the side of the bucket had a draft, and when that fire started, we would put the iron down on the bucket and it would heat. You put two irons on that, but you could use three irons at the fireplace—in the wintertime we heated the iron by the fire that was in the house. Or either you could use four irons at the fireplace, but you couldn't use that many on the coal bucket cause there wasn't room. When you take your iron off, you'd clean it off good with a rag or you'd rub your iron on a piece of cedar bush—that'll clean it up. Then you iron. Isn't that somethin! Say, Lord, Lord, we have come a long ways! But I never could iron no way. I'd iron the wrinkles out on this side and iron in on the other one.

So if we didn't go to field on Saturday, about all we'd do was wash clothes sometime and iron and sweep the yard. We didn't have no grass in the yard. If grass come on there, we'd take it and pull it up and throw it away. And we swept the yard with a brush broom. We'd go in the woods and cut dogwood bushes—they'd be branchy. We'd take those limbs and we'd tie em all together with three strings. You put one up high, one in the middle, and one way down. We kept that for our yard broom. We'd sweep the yard and the yard just as clean. We did it on Saturday so it'd be pretty for Sunday. We wanted it like that when people came to visit on Sundays.

We had flower beds out in the yard—we had a lotta flowers. My mother used to plant em on each side of the walkway in our front yard, and we used to bring flowers inside and put em in a little jar and set em on the mantle-piece. Or either we'd put a bouquet in the middle of the table in the company room—we'd do that. But we used to have a yard *fulla* flowers. We'd have these brown-eyed Susans was the main thing we'd have on each side of the walk—tall ones—and they'd bloom. They'd be so pretty. And we had rose bushes and somethin we'd call headache leaf. It had big leaves and it had pretty blooms on it. They'd be red and some be just pink. If you had a headache you'd go out there and get this leaf, put it to your head and put a rag around it to hold it on. Say good for headaches.

And I know my father used to make pine top tea and put merlin in it. Pine needles—we call em "pine top," but it's pine needles—and merlin. That made a tea for colds. Oh, boy! And peach tree leaves that made a tea for fever. You know the leaves of the peach tree, they're bitter—they're real bitter. Just like you got a temperature, you can make a tea outa that and you drink that and it'll cool the fever. And if we ever got into poison ivy we'd go to the fig tree and pull off the leaves. It's a milk in em. You didn't know it? They got milk—it's white—and it'll run out and you rub it on you. That's good for poison ivy—it grew in the woods. We'd always be in the woods cause I used to go in the woods and hunt turkeyberries. They used to grow close to the ground on a little vine. They were pink and they were sweet. That was in the spring of the year they'd come out. We'd be gettin dogwood brooms to sweep the yard and we'd get turkeyberries. We knew where they grew cause they grew in a moister place round a branch, so we'd go there, pull up them vines, and look and get those berries and eat em.

But we had quite a few different kinds of flowers in our yard. We had bridal wreaths around our porch—they'd bloom so pretty. And we had jonquils—they had yellow flowers on em. They always bloomed early and they'd be gone. You could take jonquil stems, and we used to catch jacks with them. It's some holes be in the ground in the yard—it's some things called jacks that put these holes in the ground, and they'd stay in the hole. We'd take these jonquil stems and we'd get down, we'd spit on the ground and we'd roll it round the dirt, run it down the hole and jiggle it, and he'll grab it. We'd pull him up. Oh! We used to see how many we could catch. That was somethin we used to play before we was really old enough to work in the field.

And I tell you somethin else we used to play is doodle-oodles. It would be some sand in the yard, and it'd have a sink right in the middle of it. We'd go there and we'd blow at it and say, "Doodle-oodle, doodle-oodle, come and get

your supper and draw your water 'fore it rain on you."
We'd keep blowin, and after awhile he'd come forth. I don't
know where we got that from, but we'd sing and we'd
blow and he'd come up. It's a little old brown bug—we'd
call him "doodle-oodle." Oh, brother! Those things is funny.
Now those are the kinda things that we played.

When it's hot we used to go under the house and play.
It was on blocks so we could go under it. The chickens
would go under there, too. And I remember my grandfather used to come visit and bring us some candy—that
was Stella's father and my mother's father, Grandpa Vernon. He'd bring us candy and we didn't like that kind, so
we'd go under the house and bury it. Every time he came
he'd bring candy, and look like he didn't know but one
kind to buy, and I didn't like it. So we'd go under the
house and bury that candy up under there.

We used to play with our dolls under the house. Every
Christmas the Santy Claus would bring me a doll—it would
be either a boy or a girl doll, but I'd get a doll every year.
I remember I got a big doll once and he had on rompers—
a boy doll. I'd unbutton em and take em off, and my
grandma see me put em off, she make me put em on. "Put
em on and give me that doll here!" She'd take it and put
it in her trunk. I'd play with that doll *every once* in awhile
cause she kept it in the trunk, and that doll would be just
as pretty when next Christmas come. She shoulda let me
play with it and taught me how to take care of it, but no,
she gonna be sure that I take care of it by puttin it in the
trunk! So what I would do, I would go across the field and
I would pull up a hunk of grass—big grass with long roots—
and I would plait that grass that I would play with for my
doll. Oh, boy! We didn't have nothin to play with, but

we'd make things. But when my grandmother went to stay with Rhoda and them, my mother let me play with my dolls all the time, and that's where the end of my dolls went cause I tore em up. You see, Aunt Grace was ill—Rhoda's mother was ill—so my grandmother went and stayed with them until she died, and then Rhoda and Molly come to my father's. I stopped gettin dolls then. I was about eight.

We didn't have many to play with, but I used to play with a girl named Winifred. She was the Harrisons' grand-daughter. Her mother's husband was a gamblin man, and that was a disgrace cause he got shot on the gamblin ground where he was gamblin at. Now it wasn't in Orchard because you know how people used to go from place to place gamblin. But we heard that somebody had shot him because he had won a lot of money. That was Buck Harrison's only son—he was Winifred's father. But Winifred would always come play with us. I remember one day we was playin together and we had a misunderstandin on our way from Aunt Georgia's house, and so we just started fighting, and she's whoopin and she's hollerin because I beat her up. Then I came right on by her house and Mrs. Harrison asked me, did I want somethin to eat? I told her, "Yes." So I ate dinner with her. I didn't tell it and she didn't tell it, but I ate dinner with her. Then I came on home. I never was a fighter—I'd never get into fights. But she and I, we played together, and we got on somethin that didn't agree with each other that day, so I jumped on her cause I knew I could beat her. I beat her up and I went right on home with her and ate. Oh, brother!

But me and Winifred Harrison used to play together—that was regular. And Lydia used to come and play some-

time—she was older than we were. But me and Winifred
and Emmy Lou Randolph, those were my playmates. We
didn't have nothin to do so sometime me and Rhoda and
Molly, we'd go by and get Winifred, and we used to play
"hop-a-lie." We used to take bucket lid—tum tumble umble
umble, tum tumble. You beat on the lid and dance and
sing:

> Way down yonder where the moon shine bright,
> We don't need no 'lectric light.
> Hop-a-lie, Baby. Let's get on out!

> The goose chewed tobacco, the dog drank wine,
> The monkey played fiddle on the pumpkin vine.
> Hop-a-lie, Baby. Let's get on out!

> Ever since my dog been dead,
> Your hog been rootin in my tater bed.
> Hop-a-lie, Baby. Let's get on out!

"Let's get on out!" We'd be gettin a partner then. We'd be
in a ring and I got a partner, you got a partner, everybody
got a partner. And when we'd go to sing, I'd go skippin
across the ring—I'd steal her partner and come back with
her partner. She'd go and steal somebody else's partner.
We'd just keep goin, pattin our hands and our feet and
swinging partners. Oh, boy! We would be dancin in the
moonlight. Like on Saturday night, we'd go to Lydia's
house some nights or go to Winifred's house one night
and then go to our house one night. Wasn't no boys at it.
There was Davey and Al Hawkins and Theodore Randolph—all them—but they were older than we were and
they had their own things, so they didn't follow us. Lydia's
brother Sterlin and Willie Lee Randolph come sometime,
but we were younger, so it was just us girls. We would go
from house to house and we'd get out there in the yard,

and we'd sing and steal each other's partners and just be swingin around like I don't know what.

But when we got bigger my father stopped *that*. When we got to gettin big, he wouldn't let us do nothin like that at night. Sometime we had a box supper on Saturday night. Church supper—called a box supper. They sell the supper while it's in the box when they wanted to raise some extra money for somethin. And oh, we used to fix our box! We'd have egg pie and fried chicken and biscuits and *cake*. Our boyfriends would buy our box cause we'd have good food and we wanted to get our own box. But look like one time somebody else got a hold of our box and we didn't get a chance to get it. Oh, brother! It was nice, but we didn't have em too often. Mostly we had to be at home. But one thing about it, none of us never brought any scandalous on him. We didn't have no babies, and we didn't lay around with boys kissin and huggin round in no dark places. We never did that.

But when Saturday night come, that was the big bath night. Before you go to bed you take your Saturday night bath because you gettin ready to go out for Sunday. We took our bath in the bedroom where we slept. We carried warm water from the stove and put it in the tub—the stove had a reservoir on it what we kept water hot on one side, but you wouldn't have a whole lot of it. Sometime in the summertime we set the big tub outside and we'd draw water from the well and we'd leave the water in the tub. Then when we come home in the evenin, it was just nice enough to take a bath in it without heatin it. But that water when you draw it outa the well be cold, so you had to heat it.

And it's a funny thing, we used to use barney squash

for a bath sponge. The barney squash was a yellow squash that grew on a vine. We had barney squash vines growin over one side of the porch, and my mother stringed them up. They'd be so pretty—they would hang down on the vine. You open it up and it had somethin in it like a sponge, but it was coarser. It had seeds in that part. You take that out and take the seeds out, and you can use that for a bath. They were kinda rough, and if you been bit by mosquitos and fulla chiggers, they were real good to wash with then. So that's what we used.

But I remember one Saturday night my grandmother done made us take our bath and then she told us, she say, "Listen—." My brother and I done took the bath and decided we'd play awhile. My grandmother say, "Go to bed, you all," say, "because I gotta take my bath." So we played right along and we weren't payin no attention, you know, like kids do. We just played right on. She say, "Listen, I ain't goin tell you all no more now to go to bed cause I wanna take my bath." When she said it the second time, I just looked up at her and say, "Oh, Gramma, why you want us to go to bed so bad? You must be got somethin you don't want us to see!" When I said that, Grandma beat me good! She give me a good one. Oh, brother, did she! I went on to bed then, I'm tellin you. I didn't have nothing to do but holler and go to bed!

# SIX

## *On Sundays I Wore Baby Doll Shoes*

O N SUNDAYS I wore baby doll shoes. It's a strap that come across and buttoned, and a bow on the toe. That's baby dolls! I just loved those shoes! Oh, those were the beautifullest I ever had on! My father used to buy them for me, and he would order these pretty dresses when I was small. I used to wear beautiful little dresses with a whole lotta lace to church, and they would have velvet bows and a velvet band at the waist. Oh, boy! I thought I was dressed!

But when Rhoda and them came that changed because we *all* wore the same thing—shoes, everything would be just alike—to school and to church. Peoples would say, "There go the three twins," and if you see me comin before you see them, whatever you saw me with on, that's what the others had on when they got there. So you see one, you see all of us. My father say the reason why he dressed us like that because peoples couldn't say that Will put more on his daughter and better things on his daughter than he did his sister's children. So he dressed us all alike.

I remember the boy that I really loved—that was a boy named Jamie Watts—we'd go to Sunday school together. We's call ourselves courtin. We come up together from little. His mother was sick—she had T.B. Her husband had left her, and she had three boys, but Jamie's the one looked after his mother. He was small—we all were small—but he done all the cookin, all the washin and everything what his mother's sister didn't come and do. After his mother died, his father came and got Jamie and them and carried them with him to Springfield to Watts Corner, they call it, and that's when we got separated. I didn't see him no more in a long time. I probably wasn't but 'bout twelve and a half years old or might not a been that old. But before his mother died, he lived over there not far from us, so we'd be walkin together goin to Sunday school, comin from Sunday school, and I would tote his hat and—you see now what kinda courtin! He needed his hat on his head! But I would have his hat, and he'd have my umbrella over me— Stella's mother gave me an umbrella. They were very scarce at that time among people, and I thought I was somethin! Now wasn't that silly? He would carry that umbrella over me, and I would be carryin his hat. I really liked him, but I was too young.

We'd come home from church and sometime the preacher would be there. He would come to Orchard on Saturday in order to be there to preach on Sunday, and he would stay there Saturday night, Sunday night, and go back on Monday on the train. He would go to different one of the deacon's houses and spend the night. He come to our house some Saturday night, and then next time he'd go to another deacon's home. So he used to come spend the night, and when the train come along at twelve o'clock, my father would have to go meet him at the station and bring him to the house. You know, he'd be comin from Selma. Well, that was way past us cause we didn't have nothin at our little place. You know, Orchard is a small place, so you got to Selma, you done went to town! But we had swept the yard so nice and clean and we'd have the tablecloth on the table waitin on him. And we'd be outside playin round and then we could see him comin on up the road—he would sit up there in the buggy or he'd be ridin in the car—and we'd say, "Here they come!" Oh, we'd be glad for him to come because we's gonna have some good eats, too!

My mother would fix a big meal, and I remember hearin a story that said the preacher was coming to this house once, and say that the lady's gonna kill a chicken so they could have fried chicken for the preacher cause the preacher love chicken. So she sent the kids out to run the chickens down so she'd kill a chicken. The chickens ran, ran—all of em ran down in the woods and everywhere—and this chicken outrun the one was runnin it, so they had to leave the chicken. And said old rooster was down there. When the chicken got down there, the old rooster say, "Is the preacher gone?" The rooster crowin, you know. And the guinea said, "Not yet. Not yet." That's what they sound like. My father used to tell us that story.

When it get round time for the preacher to come to our house, my mother would be done fatten the chickens in the coop and cleaned em out. My mother would always put chickens up in the coop which would be a board box with some planks on top of it. They'd all be sittin around out in the yard. And she'd clean the chickens out by givin em cornmeal—wet it and put bakin soda in it—and that would clean the chickens out. We'd put em up about a week or more—we'd always keep chickens on hand cleaned out that we'd have chickens to eat. They'd be so *good* because when you get ready to cook em, they wouldn't be runnin around in the yard and in the lot pickin up every-thing and eatin everything.

So my mother'd have fried chicken and she'd cook veg-etables and cakes and pies. The preacher and my daddy would eat first; then we'd eat what was left. And the preacher'd get on that chicken plate, and you thought he wouldn't *never* get off. Honestly, my mother just cook and cook; and the preacher would just eat, eat, eat, eat, eat; and they talk, talk, talk, talk. We wanted him to get up from the table *so* bad so we could eat. We'd be waitin, wonderin if the preacher's gonna eat the last piece! So the preacher finally got up one Sunday and he asked my brother, say, "How come you ain't eatin, Davey?" Davey say, "I'm waitin on Momma to measure the milk." Oh, boy! Momma say she coulda went through the floor. The cows had begin to not give much milk because they'se goin out—we wasn't milkin I don't think about one cow at that time—so my mother would measure the milk and give us so much and make it right for everybody. When we had plenty we just drink milk—we'd have a big churn and it'd be over half fulla milk. But at that particular time the milk was about gone, and my brother waitin on Momma to measure that out what we had. We all laughed at that a long time. Oh, brother! I look at kids nowadays—what they throw away we didn't have. We'd a been glad to get what they throw away.

So my father and the preacher would eat and we would be out on the porch just *waitin* and lookin and listenin for em to be pushin their chairs back so they can get up from the table because whatever was left, that was for us. And as I told you, we didn't know that the chicken had much but the head and the feet—that's about what we would

get. Then when we'd finish our eats, we'd sit down and
chew our bones and talk and have fun, we would, the kids
together. And the preacher and my father, they'd be up
in the company room. We didn't have no company room
until shortly after my cousins had come to live and we had
to have more rooms, and we didn't have the preacher before
that time either. But we had a bed in there, and we had
some straight chairs and a table in there, and that would
be where the preacher would stay. And in the mornin we'd
have breakfast. My mother be cooked biscuits and fried
meat which would be whiteback. We called it "whiteback"—it was a slab bacon. Or either she'd sometime kill
another chicken and have fried chicken for breakfast and
rice, biscuits, butter, syrup—have a lot on the table—and
coffee. I remember that pretty well, but that was for the
preacher.

When we got finished eatin breakfast my father would
get us off to Sunday school first, and then he and the
preacher would come on later. We'd go to Sunday school
and we'd have song and we'd have prayer and we'd have
books that we'd read. And then after Sunday school we'd
have recess, and then at that time the peoples be comin
into church. Then at eleven o'clock my father and the other
deacons would start the prayer meeting, and they would
sing hymns and pray, and then the preacher would get up
in the pulpit and he would preach the word. He'd preach
about how you would have to treat your brother and sister
like you would want to be treated yourself. And he would
talk about how you should do as you preach—those were
some of the things that he would say. And talk about you
should have love for each other cause love hides a multi-
tude of faults—if we really love a person, we can be willin

and able to forgive that person even if we have been treated wrong. Things like that.

And when the preacher preach, the peoples be sayin, "Amen. Amen." And if anybody got happy that day they'd shout—they start pattin their hands and jump up and start shoutin. That'd be when the spirit hit em, I guess, cause I have shouted, too. When you shout you go off in somethin like a trance for a few minutes—you don't know what you doin. And when you finish, you back to your senses. But you didn't shout every time they preached and it wouldn't be shoutin all over church—it'd just be a precious few shout sometime, especially near the last when the preacher be layin it out. Then when the preacher get through preachin everybody would join into singin a song and they pick up collection, and then they dismiss and we'd leave. Now that's church.

Then when we come home from church my mother would fix dinner, and we'd just eat until I'd go under the bed in the company room and go to sleep. I'd go in the company room to keep the flies from botherin me—the flies wouldn't come in there because we had glass windows on this room. All the rest of the rooms had boards. But sometimes after we would get through eatin on Sunday, Jamie Watts and his brothers would come over to my father's house and we'd play church. We'd take our chairs outa our house and make a row of seats here and a row of seats over there—we'd have them all lined up. And this would be the aisle, and someone make a table up there with boards and chairs.

Then somebody would preach. You know, we's actin as what they did at the church. So Jamie preach one Sunday and we say, "Well, if you don't know nothing else to say, just tell what you had for dinner." He said, "Greens, bread, buttermilk." You could imagine seeing that! "Greens, bread, buttermilk." We didn't have that Sunday—we'd have somethin different Sundays. But oh, I used to be a preacher! I used to *preach!* Get up there and I'd be, *"Hey,* hey man, and *glory* to *God* on *high!* Oh, *come* on *sisters* and *come* and *give* me a *hand.* Ah *ha!* And *so* and *so* and *so!"* They'd come up shakin hands and "Halleluiah! Preach on!" Oh, boy! I could preach! We be singin and preachin and goin on and shoutin. And we'd have a collection—we'd break up old plates, and that's the money. And we'd go to table—we'd be singin and struttin goin to the table. Singin and goin, go up and pay our money and come back. Now that's what we did on Sunday evening. But you see, now kids gotta go to show. We didn't know about nothing else, but we had a good time on Sunday evenin! And if it rained we were *so* disappointed.

Some Sunday evenings my father would go back to church, especially on second Sunday because he was a deacon and they looked for him to lead prayer meetings. Other than that, my father and them just sit around on the porch and talk on Sunday evening. My father always loved to talk, and he always had somethin that somebody wanted or somebody needed to borrow, so somebody's always there. Mr. Jackson would stop at the gate and they'd talk. And also my daddy would talk with Charles Tucker—that's my mother's sister's husband, Aunt Nina's husband—he'd come down. And Buck Harrison lived not too far from us. He'd come over to my father's house in the evenin some-time, but not in the workday evenings—that'd be like on a Saturday or Sunday that he'd come over—and him and my daddy would sit and talk. They would talk to each other and watch see whose crop grew the fastest. And sometime if Mr. Harrison's crop looked better than my father's, he'd get out in front of his house, he'd sing, "*Ha, ha, ah ha* ha *ha* ha." He'd be rejoicing cause his crop was doin better than ours. My daddy say, "Well," say, "Brother Buck's crop is doin all right. Now when you hear him sayin that, he's doin all right." But he was older, and he didn't have no peoples to work because wasn't nobody but Mrs. Harrison and Winifred, so he'd never make much on it— he'd make more stalks than anything.

So Mr. Harrison would come over to my father's house, and we'd be on the porch, and he'd sit and talk with my father. And at night when it get late those big hootin owls be in the woods, and one would be in one set of the woods, and be some more in another set of the woods, and they'd be talkin to each other, and my father'd listen to what the owls say and tell us. One owl would say, "I got company." And the other owl would say, "Whoo all?" He said, "Whoo Boos,and his wife, and God knows whoo all." Well, it do sound like they be sayin that. But Mr. Harrison, he was a devil, so he put it into his words like, "I've got company." And said owl over in the next woods would say, "Whoo all?" He said, "Mr. Damn and Mrs. Damn and the whole Damn family." That's what Mr. Harrison would say. Now I never heard my father cuss cause he never did curse, so he would tell us things in a way that we wouldn't say it behind him. But the owls would be in the woods, and they'd have a conversation between themselves. And one time my father told me he was walkin through the woods one day and the owl say, "Whoo's that? Whoo's that?" My daddy say, "This is Will." The owl say, "Will, I'd like to not a known you."

My father studied them kinda things—what the birds would be sayin—and he'd sit down and tell us. And some-

time we'd be out there on the porch and a woodpecker be
out there on the pine tree and he'd be peckin on the tree.
He'd peck and he'd get around and he'd peck. And my
father'd see him and he'd sing, "Peckahwood"—we'd call
em peckahwood, but they're woodpeckers. "Peckahwood, Peckahwood, what's your head doin red? The devil
stole my *derby*, and the sun done burnt my head." That's
the reason why the peckahwood's head was red. You ever
heard that? My father'd sing that song.

And he used to tell us jokes, and he used to tell us
riddles. He'd say, "Can you tell me what this is?" I
remember one riddle he told us about "There was two legs
sittin on three legs with one leg in his lap. Up jumped four
legs and snatched away one leg. Up jumped two legs and
took up three legs and made four legs bring one leg back."
And he asked, "What was it?" Now what would it be?
That was a two-legged man sittin on a three-legged stool
with a ham in his lap. Up come a dog with four legs and
he takes away the ham. And then up jumps the man on
the two legs, and he takes up the three legs and makes the
four legs bring the one leg back! Now you never would
have thought of that, would you? But he used to ask us
things like that to puzzle our minds. And we'd say, "Out
in the field's a little green house, and in the green house
is a little white house, and in the white house is a little red
house, and in the little red house is a whole lotta little
black babies. What is that?" Now you know that's a watermelon! Those were some of the riddles we used to tell.

Oh, we had a good time. We were poor, but it was a
lotta *love*—that was the best of all! We had *love* for each
other and we got along fine. Was no fussin, no fightin in
our home. No cussin or nothin like that in our home.

◇━◇━◇━◇━◇━◇━◇

# SEVEN

# We Laid By the Crop in July

ALL THIS TIME we'd have off on Saturday evenins, Sunday, and right back to work on Monday. My mother would see that we went to field on time, plus she would see that we went clean—we had to go clean even if we have on homespun dresses. Then she stayed home and cooked dinner for us. She would start preparin by goin to the garden and gatherin vegetables like okrie and string beans, and she'd carry em home in her apron and wash em. And if she had meat, she'd put the meat on early and boil the meat and she'd put vegetables in. And you know there was a lot of us so it took quite a bit of time.

So my mother always fixed our dinner, and she had her babies, and when I was small I'd have to keep up behind the little ones and help take care of them. I used to take care of them every day. My mother and them would be out workin in the field around the house, and I would take the kids out in the yard, and I'd get up in the chinaberry tree lotta times, pick chinaberries and make chains out of em for the kids with a thread and needle. And we'd play in the dirt and we'd make frog houses. You ever heard of frog houses? You dig a hole in the dirt, and you put your foot in there and pat it round your foot with your hand till it get firm, pull your foot out, and there would be a little house. Frogs would hop in it at night, and sometime we found frogs in there. Well, I'd be showin the kids that. And we'd make mud cakes. And then sometime if my mother and them was far enough off, I would take a piece of tin and two bricks and put that tin over them two bricks and make up a little fire under there, and that would be my stove. We'd cook pancakes—steal meal or flour from the kitchen and cook pancakes and eat em. My mother wouldn't know that. But if we did somethin bad and she caught it she'd say, "All right, I'm goin turn you in to your father." We know to straighten up when she said that because whatever she told my father, he would beat us. If it wasn't bad, like we's fussin at home among the kids, she'd just tell us that in order that we quit doin whatever, but she didn't tell him—she'd save us. But if we didn't stop, we'd know what was gonna be the consequence! And then my father'd tell you to sit down and he would tell you,

> Quiet as a lamb,
> Busy as a bee—
> That's the kinda children
> Peoples like to see.

I wasn't "quiet as a lamb"—I was always talkin! And they say one thing, I had somethin to match it. But I was always "busy as a bee" when I grew up, and I guess that's why I can work now. But when I was about nine I was nursin my sister Sally—I'm about seven or eight years older than Sally. And when I would put her to sleep, instead of me goin somewhere and sit down and play, I'd get my little old hoe and get out there and work right in the field around the house. I never was lazy—I always liked to work when I wasn't told. If you work when you're not told, you don't have to go beyond it unlessen you want to, and then you get praise for it—my mother would always praise you when you did somethin nice. Oh, I love her! She was very sweet to us! She really was! And she petted me a lots. I guess it was because I didn't have no momma, and I reckon she had that affection, too, towards me because she was kin to my mother. They were related because my momma Hannah used to call my grandfather Cousin Vernon, and Cousin Vernon was my mother's father, see? That's the way my momma Hannah and my father got goin together, cause my momma Hannah and my mother would visit each other, and my momma Hannah was tryin to help another lady to get my father after my mother died. And so instead of my daddy likin the lady that my mother was tryin to get my father to court, he liked her. So that's the way they got married. But my mother petted me and I think she liked me very much—I do believe that—and still do.

But I always liked praise, and every time I'd do somethin they praise me, I'd do more. One day Davey and Rhoda say, "You just keep on," say, "you better be tryin to not work," said, "because one of these days when you get bigger," say, "you gonna have to go to work anyhow." "I don't care," I would tell them. "I don't care." So I put myself out there, and I went to doin pretty good job until they put me in the field. But oh, boy! When I did have to go every day, I wished I was home!

I was about eleven years old when I stayed out workin in the fields all day. But on a rainy day when it done rain too much to go out in the field to do anything, we'd sit out on the porch and *if* we had somethin to sew, we'd do that. In the summertime if it done rained, we'd sit on the porch and make our work dresses—we'd make about two dresses every three months to work in the field. My mother would go to town to get us material—it's a material that they call homespun—rough and tough. It would sometime be striped—our convict clothes! If it wasn't, it mighta been plain, but mostly it was striped. Never was no gay flowers or nothin. So that's what she would get for our work dresses, and she would cut it out for us, and we would make em ourselves. But I never could sew—I never did have patience enough to sew. I would hurry up and I'd be the first one to get finished because I'd make long stitches. Then I'd say, "I'm through, you all. Lookee here!" And my mother would look at it, she'd say, "Take it loose." She'd make me take it out and do it again.

My mother'd be sitting there on the porch and she'd be sewing, too. She'd sew all our sheets and pillowcases. My father used to go down to Mr. Brantley's and get twenty-four-pound sacks of flour, and she'd make our pillowcases outa those. Sometime he'd buy two sacks of flour so we'd have two pillowcases just alike when we get through usin the flour. Then my mother'd buy unbleached domestic— that's a yellow-lookin material, but it's real strong. She'd make pillowcases outa that. And unbleached domestic sheets—they would be made by my mother with a seam down the middle. They rough, but they last a long time. Or either my mother'd be sitting there patchin clothes. I never could patch. Shoo! When I get through, it'd be ready to fall off. But if we didn't do that we'd piece up quilts— we'd help my mother do that, too. She'd give us some scraps and we'd cut squares and sew em together. But I never could sew and I never could use a thimble, so I'd make a long stitch so that needle wouldn't stick in my fingers. But Momma, she would tell us if we didn't learn how to sew and cook and wash and clean, when we'd grow up and get married and have our own children, we wasn't gonna know anything and nobody wasn't gonna put up with us. She'd tell us things like that. So I learned how to cook cause I always liked to eat and I like to cook. But I don't really like to iron! I don't like to sew!

When it rained, my mother would have us sewin sometime, or she would make us wash that day, but all I wanted to do was go fishin. Oh! I *loved* to go fishin! So if it rained and we couldn't work in the field, we'd do the housework in the mornin and go to fishin in the evenin. And when we worked, it was just *fine* for us to have to work beside a place that was a branch that had fishes! We'd fish all day—we'd rush down there to see what's on the hook. I'd always carry my hook, and you know you can always dig worms up when you workin in the field, so we saved them worms. Or we'd break open an old rotten wood and get wood sawyers—we used to fish with them. So I'd slip off from the field and take the kids and go fishin.

If we caught any fish, we'd break off a long twig with a fork on it—you'd have one fork and another one. You'd put the fish on there between the two forks and you'd stick it down in the bank and they'd stay fresh in the water all day. So we'd catch little fish and we'd take em home. If they was a perch we'd scrape em, and if they was a cat we'd skin em off. Then we'd fry em and just eat em. They were good. Fish was really exceptional because we had pork and we'd have beef, we'd have chicken. But when you get fish, that was something that we didn't have too often unless we went to fishin. But oh, brother! They'd know we'd been if we carried fish home, so we had to tell a story about we just had our hooks set and while we was workin, we'd go see about the hooks. I'm tellin you, I'm gonna die now to get down South and go to fishin!

But we didn't get to fish too often because we's always busy in the field, and sometime we'd work in somebody else's field, too. We used to work for a white man up there not too far from us—his name was Garrett. We would be hoein in the field—cornfield we'd hoe or we'd hoe in the cotton field for him sometime. And then we would pick cotton for him. That's when we'd be caught up with our own, they would hire us to come and we'd work. And did you know we used to go up there and work for fifty cent a day? Hoe *all day long* for fifty cent! Then lotta time we'd turn that into syrup, a gallon of syrup. Each one would let his fifty cent go for a gallon of syrup to carry home because ours would be practically runnin out. There's me and Rhoda and Molly, so that would be three gallons right there to bring home. Or either we'd get corn when ours was about gone because it was a certain time of the year when weevils gets into the corn, so then you start feedin it up for the hogs pretty well.

So my father would let us go and work for Mr. Garrett, and that'd add more to it. And my mother, she didn't do much work out because she would cook, and it always was the little ones to look after, so she'd be looking after them. But she used to go up there and wash, and sometime they would give her a jar of cracklins for her day's wash. Now isn't that somethin? But that's all they'd have to give us because money was as scarce with them I guess as it was with us pretty near. But they musta thought they was more than we were because when we'd go to the spring to get water, Mr. Garrett had to drink the water first. See, if we wanted water we just tell him, "I'm going get some water"—never just but one go. Mr. Garrett wouldn't say nothin. But when you bring it back, then he's thirsty and he'd holler, "Water boy, bring the water round. If you don't like your job, set your bucket down." Mr. Garrett would be teasin, you know, but that mean bring it on to him. So we'd take it to him first—we knew—and then he'd drink and his kids would drink and then we'd drink. And I didn't like that, and I said to my father, "I don't like to be drinkin behind Mr. Garrett and them." Then my father always was kinda afraid of my bein around white peoples because he knew that if anything came up wrong, I was gonna speak it. So he was constantly tellin me, "Daught, you don't go around the white folks talkin—you just keep your mouth closed. Just go over there and go to work." And if I hadda said somethin, Rhoda and them woulda come back and told it and my father was gonna tend to me—*he* was goin to do the beatin. So it took all my power not to tell Mr. Garrett, "Why you got to drink before we drink when we done went after the water?" And I'd look at him and I'd say to myself, "I don't know why we didn't bring our own bucket to get our own water." And I would be glad to go get the water cause I'd drink mine at the spring.

So Mr. Garrett thought he was up above us, but he wasn't because he wore common clothes just like we did. And they had a board house with a well on the outside like we did. Just wasn't a bit better'n ours. And then if he hadn'ta been poor, when he had somebody to work for him, he could give em money instead of givin em corn and syrup. And he wouldn'ta been livin where he was livin— he was livin among the colored peoples. So they was white and they didn't have no more than we had and they didn't look no better than we did—just a different color, that's all. But we knew they were poor.

And we were poor, too, but after all my father had a big family and it took quite a bit to feed us, you know. So we pretty near raised what we needed, but sometime at the end time it started runnin out. But instead of lettin it run all out, we'd get out and work—to keep that goin—to Mr. Garrett's field. And if we went, my father didn't let us do like the kids do now. The kids go and do a little work now and their parents don't see the money. But if we got some money we didn't see it. My father did the collectin cause he always provided for what we needed. So that's the way that went.

We wouldn't hardly work but one or two days out in nobody's field at a time because we had plenty to do of our own. But by July the Fourth we'd mostly be finished up in the field hoeing, and then we'd have a big day because we'd be finished with our biggest work until time come then for us to pick cotton. We didn't have no recreation or no 'musement parks, but on the Fourth of July people would be playin ball and they would have refreshment stands to sell lemonade five cent a glass and homemade ice cream. There'd be a lotta boys and girls up around the school— that's where it would be. But we hardly went—my father didn't let us go. He let Davey go. On the Fourth of July Davey'd go up to the ball game, maybe sometime he might be playin. But we didn't go—very seldom we ever went to anything. We'd work half a day in the field on the Fourth of July and then, when we'd get through, we'd be lookin forward to the ice cream my mother would make for us. My daddy would go downtown and buy us a block of ice and wrap it up in wool and carry it home in the wagon and bury it in the dirt to keep it from melting so fast so we could make ice cream in our ice cream freezer what you turn. And we'd have lemonade, and my mother would cook a cake and have fried chicken. It was at home but it'd be good and we wasn't buyin it, you know what I mean?

And if you'd planted early and had good luck with them, you had a nice ripe watermelon for July the Fourth. Sometime you plant em early and cold weather kill em, but if you had some for the Fourth, from then on you'd have watermelon. We used to go in the wagon and pick the watermelons and bring em home. We had a big old barrel sittin out there by the well, and we'd put couple of watermelons in this barrel and draw cold water and put on em and let em sit in there so long. Then we'd take em and my father always cut em in big long slices, and they'd be *so* good and so *sweet*. We'd eat about two at one time, you know, the crowd.

My father used to raise lotta watermelon. He'd put these seeds in a mound—he'd put one here and put one down there. I never planted any, but I remember one time when I used to go to the spring to get water, and I used to watch a vine grew in the pasture. It grew and grew and grew. Finally it had a watermelon on it. I watched that watermelon and I nursed that watermelon and I kept it hid—I'd break branches and hide it. When it grew up and got big, I'd go by there ever so often, thump it, you know, to see if it sound like it was ripe. One day I pulled it and I ate that watermelon. Then I had a time!

So we laid by the crop in July which mean you got all the grass from it and you waitin on the cotton to bloom. My daddy didn't care then about us goin to fishin, that is, *if* my mother didn't have somethin for us to do at home.

But my daddy always gonna find something for us to do. We would have dried peas to pick after we laid by the crops—you know, we'd go in the pea patch and pick peas. You had to get the peas off because if they dried up and stayed on the vine awhile, the pods bust open and the peas spill out. So we'd pick sacks of peas and put them up for winter in the shed of the crib. Then when my mother say she gonna cook peas for dinner in the wintertime, she'd go out there to the shed, or either she'd send us and we'd go out there and get so many peas in a sack. Then we'd get a stick and beat that sack—boom, boom, boom—and the peas'll shell themselves. Then we take the hulls out and give em to the cows cause the cows could eat them. When the peas were over, the cows would eat the vines, too. But when we get down to nothin but the peas and the little fine stuff, then you just put em in a pan and take the pan and shake it up and down till you get em all cleaned out. When you get em cleaned out, you wash em and then you boil em. That's the way we did peas.

And we'd pull the fodder from the corn long about the same time we'd gather peas. That's in order to feed the cows and the mules in the wintertime. So we'd pull the blades off the stalk when they start turnin brown. You can't pull fodder when it gets too dry because it's too brittle and it breaks, so you have to pull it when it's half dried and half green. Then you tie it in little bunches—hands—and you bend the stalk down and you break the top of the stalk off and you hang em on the stalks until they dry. Then it's time for you to go back and put four of those hands together and make a bundle, and you throw it down, make heaps in between the rows. Then you come along with the wagon and the mules and gather that up and haul it to the fodder stacks. My father cut a small pine tree for his pole and he put it in the ground and he stacked this fodder around that pole—it'd be close around the crib somewhere—and he'd take fodder from the fodder stack and give it to the mules in the lot. So that's done—it's finished before you pick cotton.

But you leave the ears of corn stand on the stalk. The corn didn't go into the crib until after the cotton was ginned because the cotton had to stay in the crib. The last thing to gather is the corn, unless you have velvet beans what you feed the cows in the wintertime and sugar cane to make your syrup and the shinny. But when that corn goes to dryin out, then that's the time to gather it and load it on the wagon and put it in the crib.

The crib was in the lot, and the lot had a big gate to it. When my father'd get ready to put this corn in the crib, he would open this big gate in order that he bring the wagon in. The pigs was in the lot runnin around, so one time he called me and he say, "Come here, Daught." He told me, "I want you to mind these pigs. You keep the pigs back. Don't let em come outa the gate." Say, "If they try to come out of there, you *kill* em." But he really didn't mean for me to *kill* em, you know. So I was keepin the pigs back with a little pole and all for certain one of the little pigs came runnin up there and slid by the gate. When the pig came out I did just what he say—I took and I hit that pig. That pig went off squealing and draggin his two back legs cause I done broke him down. My father jumped down off the wagon and he got a big old peach tree switch and he *give* it to me. I said, "Well, you told me to kill the pig." He said, "Well, I thought you had better sense."

So there wasn't much to do in August except pick peas

and pull fodder, and revival would start in August. It'd just be different churches would call themself havin a revival meeting to save souls, they said, by sinners comin and joinin the church. The revival would start on Sunday and go to that Friday and the preacher would come into town from Selma or Birmingham and he would stay the whole week long. Then they'd have a meeting every night singin and prayin and preachin and takin up collection and takin in mourners which would be the sinners sittin on the mourners' bench. That's the front bench in the church, you know, but revival's the only time it's called the mourners' bench. And then when the preacher get through preachin, he'd just hold out his hand and be askin the mourners to "Come give me a hand and God your heart." Then if you wanted to come and join the church, you go up there and give the preacher your hand, and he'd shake it and you'd sit down in front of the pulpit. I sat on the mourners' bench a lotta times when they'd have revival— sat on there all the week. But when I got tired of sittin on the mourners' bench, I joined the church, and after that I didn't sit there no more. I was around eleven.

So the revival has gone on all week and on Friday night, that's the last meeting, so then on Saturday all those that wanted to join the church would be baptized. So you go to the pool—it was down the hill from the church cause there was a stream of water down there and the pool was at the stream. You go to the pool and they had a little board house—you go in there and you change your clothes into a gown and you tie your head up with a scarf and you come out. And then they'd be singin, "Let's go down to the water . . . ," and it'd be a deacon help you down the two steps to the preacher down in the water. Then the preacher would say, "I baptize you, my sister, in the name of the Father and of the Son and of the Holy Ghost. Amen." Then you fold your arms across your chest, and the preacher take you by your shoulder and dip you back in the water and bring you up, and it was a deacon help you come outa the pool.

But I've been baptized twice cause when I became a Jehovah's Witness, it was a white man baptized me and, boy, did I feel good when I come outa *that* water. That was in '75. You see, I always used to go to church and listen to the preacher cause I would love to sing in the choir and I would just like to be there and be with other peoples. That's what I was going to church for, mostly, because I never would sit down and read the Bible. And I thought if you got the religion and be baptized that you wouldn't go to hell and burn in the fire forever. But I've learned since I've been a Jehovah's Witness that a preacher that preach like that—what the peoples wanta hear—that's ticklin their ears. So I was goin to get my ears tickled. But now I love to go to Jehovah's Witness and the reason why I love it is we learn the Bible, and then not only learn it for ourselves, but we learn to not be selfish with what we learn and we go and tell others in order that they might learn too, and that is accordin to what the Bible say do. That's what I'm doin.

But we was raised up going to church and we would go from one church to the other one durin that revival time because they'd have all of August for revivals waiting to pick the cotton. And we didn't go every evenin to the other churches, but we'd practically go every evening to *our* revival because my father was a deacon. So we'd work in the daytime in the field and come home and wash up, and we'd get on that wagon and we'd get goin to that meetin in the evenin. The smaller children would sit up front with the older people so they wouldn't fall off, or my mother'd take an old quilt and make a pallet in the wagon and let em lay down there—some of em would be to sleep when you get to church. And the bigger children would sit on the board across the back, and if we didn't have the board to sit on, we'd sit on the floor of the wagon with all our legs hangin out.

So my father would hitch up the mules and we'd go in the wagon. All those who wanted to go went. But my sister Essie and I, we'd go sometime. When we felt like stayin home and kill a chicken, we'd stay home and kill a chicken and fry roastin ears. We'd send the little ones away like, "Go over to Mrs. Harrison and see if she got. . . ." We'd ask for somethin that we'd know Mrs. Harrison didn't have in order to get them away from the house. Just as soon as we knew that they was outa sight, me and Essie would start callin the chickens. When the chickens come, the one that we thought oughta be fat and heavy, we got him, you know. So Essie and I would get a chicken and kill the chicken and clean and fry this chicken.

And we'd have fried corn—we'd go to get roastin ears out there in the cornfield at the house and fry it. We'd have early corn that we called sweet corn for our roastin ears. And we'd have our old field corn—crib corn—that we'd plant to have through the winter to feed the hogs and the mules and the chickens and take to the mill to grind for meal. So we'd take the roastin ear and you take a real sharp knife and go down the ear once—you halvin the grain. Then you go down again and get the other half. Then you put it in a skillet with some lard—this lard from our hogs—and you put a little sugar in it to make it a little sweet and fry it until a crust under it. And boy, that would be the best! Just fry corn and cook chicken. Oh, we had the best time! This piece yours and this one mine, and this your piece and this my piece. We'd eat up that whole chicken. I'm tellin you, that was terrible! We did though.

And we used to make candy. Oh boy! We used to make *fudge* with sugar and butter and chocolate and peanuts and sweet milk. We'd make fudge and we'd be eatin fudge around there, but the rest of the group didn't know anything about it!

So they used to go to the meetin—they was gettin religion by servin God—and Essie and me, we stayed home and ate fried corn and fried chicken. But Essie told one of the others, and the others told my mother, and that broke that up. Oh, I used to be a *devil* when I was home, I be frank. I've done a lots, so that is the reason why I know like I know now, and I knows better. I've done things, but nothin bad—I never did nothin bad like girls do. I never did that, *never!* Me or none of the other kids.

So they'd have this revival all the week except Saturday, and on Sunday would be the big meeting. Aunt Mary—that's my mother's aunt—she was *old* lady, and she would always come down and stay with somebody that lived somewhere near that church where the big meeting was gonna be. So one time when I was small she come down to my father's house, and then she wanted to go to church that Sunday with Aunt Grace—that's Rhoda and Molly's mother—because the big meeting was gonna be at their church, at Horizon. So she wanted me to go with her to Aunt Grace's, and I didn't want to go with her. So, "Oh, you just come on here, gal"—she always called me "gal." "Come on here, gal. You can go." And Momma say, "Oh, go ahead on—go ahead on with Aunt Mary." And I went with her. I wasn't supposed to go nowhere but to Rhoda and them's house—I went to play with Rhoda and them. But when we got there, they had gone to the church. I didn't go there to go to church—I was barefeeted and I didn't have on the things that I would wear to church—but Aunt Mary carried me right on. When I got to church, I wouldn't sit down—I wouldn't sit down if I weren't properly dressed. I just stood up. She'd pull on my dress tail and she'd be, "Oh, sit down, gal." I'da been better to sit down outa the way so nobody see me, but I wouldn't. I didn't sit down—I wouldn't! They told my father, and he didn't give me a lickin, but he give me a good talk. But I was so stubborn that Sunday! Peoples was gettin up givin me the seat, and I stood up because I wasn't supposed to go to church barefeeted, and I just had on a plain dress, and she carried me on. I was mad. I wouldn't sit down!

But we'd go to the big meeting on Sunday, and you'd invite other peoples from different churches to come and eat. Then the peoples would turn out and bring dinner and spread their food out on the ground. So my mother would take her tablecloth, and where she's gonna spread her food, she'd put her cloth. And she used to cook chicken pies and potato pies and egg pies. Those egg pies would be so good—that butter'd be standin on top. And she would cook cake and she would cook beans—string beans or butter beans—and okrie. And she'd have a *big* box or either she'd take the trunk. Then we'd eat till there wasn't no *end* because this one'll be good, and I want some of Sister Hannah's so and so, and you get through and you have a whole plate. Oh, boy! That was a good time going then! And all the rest of the evenin we'd walk and court up and down the path goin toward the spring down there where they had the baptism pool. We'd go down to the spring and get water and back and forth and your boyfriend be walkin with you and you'd be talkin. You'd be courtin, then. But we wasn't allowed to get in nobody's car, I can tell you that! We didn't go car ridin, nothin like that. Uhn, uhn! We stayed on that church yard!

Then we'd come home in the evenings—I was courtin when I was twelve years old and I wasn't allowed to, but I called myself courtin because Molly and Rhoda was older than I was and they could have company, so I would let this boy walk with me and my two cousins because they were courtin cousins of his. I would walk on with him till I'd be nearly about home, and when I got nearly about home, I would get ahead. So this boy—I married him, too. I married him—he just kept coming on. He'd come onto the house and he'd be sitting with the others talkin. But when I get to the house, my mother'd put me to washin dishes or make me look after the little ones, and they'd be in the company room, so every chance I would get, I would run in there with the baby on my hip and say a few words and run back out cause I wasn't allowed to be courtin. I was twelve years old at that time, and my cousin Molly— that was the oldest—when she was about eighteen, she married.

So we didn't really go no place, we didn't do nothin, we didn't have nothin—and it was *hard*. Now kids got everything, they go everyplace, do whatever they want, and still—not happy. I oftentime think, "Oh, I just wish some of this time coulda been back there." Honest to God, from then till now, it's just like heaven should be. But I guess it was better for us at that time—we was happy.

# EIGHT

<><><><><><><><><><>

# *Pickin Cotton Was the Tiredest Thing*

B Y THE MIDDLE of August the cotton bolls'll start
openin up, and you start pickin the cotton about
the first of September. So then we just run and go—
hit and go, I say—because the cotton was ready and the
peas are still drying on the vines. So we'd have to hurry
up and try to pick the cotton and get all that what was
open. All of em didn't open at once, so you'd have to get
that what's open because if a wind storm come, it would
ruin the cotton, or either if it rained on it a long time, the
cottonseeds would come up inside of the boll—they'll sprout
and come up. So we'd have to try to keep up with the
cotton, and then we'd be back to the pea patch to gather
more peas. So that was *overtime* work *all* the time until
we'd get everything under control.

I'm tellin you, I have worked. You may think I'm kid-
din, but you shoulda seen me—I worked in my life! But
oh, I'd hate when that cotton started to open! Pickin cotton was the tiredest thing! You had to stoop down all the
time and pick it and put it in the sack hangin on your side.
And then when you move, you gotta pull the sack. Then
when it get full, you have to go way over and put it in the
basket and then come back. That stoopin with the sack
hung on your back, draggin up and down the row! Oh,

that was the most tiresome thing I ever seen!

You empty the cotton in these baskets—my father used to make these baskets. Then you get on it and pack it, put more in and pack it and you weigh it up. We had some scales, and the scale had a big hook on it you'd catch on a tree limb, so you'd weigh up the cotton on these scales. Rhoda picked a hundred pounds by noon and she probably picked two hundred in a day, but I couldn't pick hardly a hundred in a day. I couldn't pick cotton. I hated that cotton pickin business so bad! I'm so glad now that I learnt not to cheat, but I would cheat when I'd go off to pick some cotton at other people's place. I'd pull off the green bolls and wrap them in the cotton. And cockleburs—them sticky balls that grow on a bush—I'd pull them off, even, and wrap them up in the cotton so it'd make it weigh.

Oh! I was *really* not a cotton picker! I couldn't, really! Those little stickers on the boll always got into my fingers—if the boll is not open wide, they stick you in the finger when you try to pull the cotton out—and my fingers would be *so* sore. I *never* liked to pick cotton! I don't mind hoein—to hoe in the field, I carried the head row. I was always ahead of everybody in the hoein cause when I get my row out, I go back and help somebody else and get them out. But when it come to that cotton pickin I cheated, and I know I cheated. So I would have more green bolls in my cotton, and look like because I cheated, I still never had up to what the other peoples had cause maybe I was spendin up too much time wrappin up the bolls. I was always worried about how to cheat to have the number but not do the work. I was bad! Oh, tryin to make a dollar! Cause it was about seventy-five cent a hundred. Oh, you'se gettin good money if you got seventy-five cent for a hundred pounds. But outa all the cockleburs and all the cotton bolls, I couldn't make a hundred in a day. Pickin cotton! And those stickers would stick in your *fingers*. You'd go home and pick em out—be just as sore!

But you weigh the cotton, and then you put it in the wagon and take it home and throw it in the crib till the crib gets too full to put any more cotton in it. Then my father'd take out the wagon and put side planks on the wagon up high and the end gate, and we'd load this cotton on the wagon. He'd pack it as we throwed the cotton there. He'd pack it, pack it until he'd get all the cotton that he could get on this wagon. Then he'd take it to the gin and have it ginned. He'd haul a bale today and a bale tomorrow and a bale the next day. Maybe sometime he'd haul two bales a day cause we have made at least fifteen bales in a year.

But sometime we didn't make it much, so that's a bad year. The boll weevils would sting the square and they would turn yellow. When they turn yellow, we wasn't gonna have no cotton cause all of em would fall off, so we used to have to go round and pick up these squares and put em in a sack and my father would burn em. We'd pull em off the cotton stalk, too, and burn em. We'd be tryin to kill the boll weevil, and you could catch maybe one or two at a time, but, I mean, there're so many of em that you wouldn't catch em. They made a song about the boll weevil—they had a record—say, "I looked out and I saw the boll weevil, he's sittin on the square. Next time I looked, *all* his family was there!" They was *real* bad one year—boll weevils likely ate up everything that year and we didn't make that much cotton. When you don't make a lotta cotton like that, you had to go and take up things at the store, and then you'd be 'pendin on workin next year and payin off this which you be done took up durin the wintertime that you wouldn't have to do if you hadda made a good crop. So those were bad years, but if you have rain and time and good season, it would be a good year.

But we didn't miss it hardly—we'd make a lotta cotton. And soon as it was ginned and baled up, my father would sell the bale. Wasn't gettin nothin for it—nine, eight cent a pound. When you get ten cent a pound, you gettin some money then! But you workin, and you was just givin it away!

My father would sell the bales and the money that he got outa this, he would get his debt paid up first. You see, he would get his advancement down at the store before farming time came, and he would take up all the fertilizer he'd need. And if he needed plows or plowstocks and mule collars and mule plow lines, he'd take them up, and groceries and whatever it took to help him along until his crop is made. And when you taken up down there at the store somebody would come out in a car and my father would say, "Well, they lookin over the crops." They would always ride out and see if it's promisin enough to let you keep on takin up. Then at the end of the year when you harvest your crop, they get theirs first, and if there's any money left, you get it, and if there isn't, you just bill it up for the next year where you done took things up at the store. I'll tell you, at that time the black people, they didn't have nothin, and they couldn't get much, and if they got a little somethin, sometime it was taken from you. Cause I know they used to say at that time,

> Aught's an aught,
> And a figure's a figure.
> All for the white man,
> And nothin for the nigger!

What they mean, when the end of the year come and he get through figurin it out—what you owe him—you don't get nothin. You just worked, and the white man gets.

So we didn't have nothin much outa that cotton to depend on unless it was the seed money. My father'd sell the seeds all exceptin the ones he's gonna plant—he'd save some to plant—and then he would buy our school clothes and school shoes and whatever was needed at the house. So whatever the cottonseed come in, that's what we had.

After the cotton was gathered and the cotton was sold, then the next thing we would do, we would pull up the peanuts—pinders—so they could be put away. When we pulled the peanuts up outa the ground, we had to do that by back and hand stoopin. We pulled up the peanuts and we'd turn em bottom side with the peanuts up in order that they would dry. And if the rain come along shortly after we did that, it would wash all the dirt off em and when they dry, they'd be so pretty and clean. Then they'd go along with the wagon, take in the peanuts and put em in the crib with the pitchfork. And when it be cold and rainy and we don't have anything to do, we'd go in the crib and shell peanuts and sack em up, and we'll have these to parch in the wintertime. "Roastin" they call it now, but we called it "parch" at that time. We'd sit around the fire at night and we'd parch peanuts. We'd cook big pans full and everybody go to gettin em and eatin em. And we'd play "Jack-in-the-bush." I say, "Jack-in-the-bush," and you say, "Cut em down." I say, "How many?" If you said,

"Four," and if I got four in my hand, I have to give them
to you. And if you said, "Three," then you had to give to
me. That's what we'd play with the peanuts in the wintertime. Or sometime we'd take a little bag of peanuts to school
for lunch. But peanuts were somethin that we really
cherished.

By the time the peanuts would be put away, it'd be
time then to dig the potatoes—we had to dig sweet potatoes. You know, sweet potatoes grows in the ground
somethin like a carrot, but they're on a vine. The potatoes
is grown big enough to eat in August, so in August you
can start grabbin em—we call "grabbin" the potatoes.
Between the garden and the house it was a field that we
had potatoes to grab. Sometime the ground would crack
open around a vine—you know there'd be a big one there.
So you grab as many as you want, but you don't *gather*
those potatoes until October. My father would plow the
vines off with a shovel plow—that's a half a turn plow.
For as long as they were green, we'd throw those vines
over for the cows to eat because they liked to eat potato
vines. And when he get through takin all the vines off,
he'd go down the row deep and plow up the potatoes, and
then we had to go along and pick these potatoes and you
put em in a sack and pile em up. You had to keep runnin
to the pile to empty your sack to keep from havin to tote
such a heavy sack. When you get all the potatoes up and
piled, then my father will come around with the wagon
and take em and they make banks and put em in.

My father'd dig a big round hole in the ground. Then
you get some straw from the woods—pine straw—and
you'd line the bank with this pine straw. Then you put the
potatoes on the straw. Then you would take corn stalks—

we cut the corn stalks—and stand these stalks all the way around these potatoes like a teepee. And then you would put boards over that—lay the boards overlapping so that it wouldn't rain in the bank—and they left a place would be a door where you could move it back and get potatoes out of it. We used to cook em in the fireplace—cover em with coals, and oh, those potatoes would be so sweet till it look like honey runnin out of em whenever you bake those. They'd be so good—you just don't know! Oh! We're not livin—we're just makin time!

So the potatoes'll stay in there and stay dry all winter, and we just ate potatoes out of the tater bank. We'd have a lot of em—we've had five, six, and sometime seven or more tater banks. They'd be right behind the house outside of the palins. And then we'd have this rail fence laid that the hogs couldn't get into them. In the summertime the hogs was locked in the lot in order that they don't mess up the crops. But in the wintertime after you done gathered all the crops, we'd turn out the hogs we're going to keep that they might get all the stray potatoes that you didn't pick up and all the peanuts that they could find. And hickory nuts—they'd go in the woods and they'd eat hickory nuts. That helped to feed the hogs. They'd stay loose all winter, but they'd come back at night and we'd give em slop from the kitchen and my father fed em corn from the crib. But he didn't keep a lot of em over the winter, you know, cause he raised pigs and they'd come for the next year.

So harvest begins around the last of August, and all of September you'd be picking cotton and peas and pulling peanuts and digging potatoes. Then too, you had to gather in your fruit. We had some apple trees and some peach trees in the potato field, and they had fruit on them. We used to dry the apples—put em on a board and dry em in the sun—and my mother would put em in a flour sack. We'd make pies out of em. They good—they have all that *tang* in em. And my mother used to make jelly from the apple peels.

My mother didn't can apples, but she used to can the peaches—she used to make pickled peaches and can peaches. Davey and I used to get one out of every jar—instead of eating a whole jar, we'd get one out of each jar so she wouldn't miss it. But she did, and I would tell a story and he would tell the truth. He promised not to tell it but he did, and she'd give us a good scoldin.

But we used to have a lotta fruit. In front of the house was some plum trees—we'd have red plums and yellow plums. Oh, boy! All them plums! And fig tree and pear tree. The fig tree was behind the kitchen; then the pear tree was there. My father set out that pear tree when I was small. The pears didn't get ripe until around September, but we used to start eatin them before that—we'd steal em off the tree. It wouldn't be because my mother didn't want us to have the pears, but she knew that they were green and we would have stomach aches. We would steal em off and eat them anyway. Then when the pears start gettin ripe, I used to get up in the tree and eat the pears—I'd eat every yellow one I'd see. They would be so nice and mellow.

But when the fruit got ripe, my mother'd tell us to stay away from the fruit until she give it to us because she wanted to can. And she'd go away, and I'd go and I'd gather me up a lot of it. I'd go down in back of the well, sit down, and I would eat fruit. I just eat pears and apples.

I'm tellin you! The others didn't do like I did—they wasn't like me. I wasn't bad, but I was mischievous. But oh, boy! I loved it! I see myself just visitin from one tree to another— kinda like in the Garden of Eden!

# NINE

<><><><><><><><><>

# *We's Fixin to Kill a Hog*

BY THE TIME October came, that's the time we'd go to school. The first school I went to was on the Montgomery Hill. The reason why it was called Montgomery Hill, the peoples what lived there was all Montgomerys. And Randolphs. And the Sinbad Store was on the Montgomery Hill; Uncle Sinbad was a Montgomery himself. I remember some mornings we'd stop at Uncle Sinbad's store and buy us a stick of peppermint on our way to school. My father'd give us a nickel to buy somethin. He wouldn't give every one of us a nickel and it wasn't often, but we'd ask him and sometimes he'd give us one to buy somethin that evenin. But we couldn't wait till the evenin to spend it because, you know, to have a little money, it'll burn you, so we'd hurry up and get rid of it. But other than that, we'd go on to the school in the mornin.

It was just a boarded school—boards outside and boards inside and benches for seats. No desks. And the teacher at that time was Miss Beulah Hinton, and she had a table and had a little hand-bell on it. We'd get to the school in the morning and the bell would ring and we'd get in line and walk in. And all of us what went to school there was in one room—it was a one-room school.

I started goin to school there when I was seven years

old and I went to that school at least two years. Then the crowd went to gettin too big for that little school, so they built this other school and we kept on goin there. The school that they built was a three-room school, and from time to time they built onto the school. It was up on the highway and we'd have to walk to school and back home—my brother and me, and Rhoda and them when they came.

But we would go to school in the fall, and then we'd come in from school in the evenin and we'd scrap the cotton. We'd be gettin the last bolls. You could see a boll opening here and over there—here and there—so you just be goin where you see a boll. I hate to scrap cotton because you'd do so much walkin for such a little, but sometime you'd be gettin pretty good with a whole big sack. Then sometime you turn the cows out and they eat the leftover bolls what didn't open and the leaves off the cotton after we get through scrappin.

My father would take this scrap cotton to the mill and have it ginned, and he'd give my mother the cotton, and she'd get this ticking and make a new mattress and fill it fulla this fresh cotton. She'd make one or two new mattresses each year, and we had pillows outa cotton just like that, and my mother would always make quilts—she'd pad them with scrap cotton. We had plenty quilts and we stayed *warm.*

Our beds was wooden beds, and they'd have a spring, and a mattress next to the spring, and another mattress on top of that. When we'd make the bed we'd be pat, pat— some of em could make it so level. And we'd put all the covers on it—the bed would be so *soft.* But my two cousins that my father raised and I, we three slept in a bed together. All the beds were full because it was a lot of us, you know.

And the old mattresses get knotty if you don't get there and pull em apart and whup em and beat em and make em rise, so any time we took a notion, we'd take the mattresses out in the good old hot sun and beat em and air em all day. It would freshen em up.

And we used to have bed bugs. They'd lay the eggs in every little crack in the bed because we didn't have paint, and they would hatch out and there'd be a lotta little bugs. They'd eat you at night. They were real bad one time—those things wouldn't even let you sleep. But we finally got rid of em because after so long we'd take down the beds, we'd take those beds outside, and we would wash those beds off in hot scalding water. We'd put hot water all around the beds and those slats. And my mother'd wash the mattresses. She'd spread a sheet or an old quilt on the ground, and she'd open the mattresses up and empty out all the cotton, and she'd wash the mattresses and boil em and hang em up to dry. When the mattresses dry we'd put the cotton back in, sew em up, and put em back on the beds, and that was good sleepin. We'd do that in the springtime when the sun be shinin and the air be fresh and cool. But I remember one time we'd put em out and Momma had pulled all the cotton outa the mattresses on a big old spread, and she washed the mattresses, and before the time we got ready to put the cotton back in, a great storm came. We just grabbed the spread up on each side and we was tryin to bring the cotton in the house, but all this cotton blew all over the yard and come up on the porch and everywhere. Oh, boy! We was grabbin cotton and rakin cotton. It was somethin!

So we'd come home from school and scrap cotton. We'd be tired, but when we'd get through scrappin, we'd have a little snack. Nowadays kids'll go for an ice cream or a soda pop which would be somethin that they really like to have, but in the country we'd eat accordin to what come along. When berries come along we'd have berries, and when plums come along we'd have them. And then we'd have sugar cane in the fall—if we come by the cane field on our way home, we'd have that for our little snack. Sometime we'd eat it up before we got home so nobody wouldn't know we'd been in the cane patch, and we'd hide the top out there in the woods. You see, it was too far to go to the cane patch from the house unless it was Saturday, but sometime on Saturdays we'd go and get five or six stalks of cane. We would take it home and we'd stand it in what we call our little room closet—it was a little room on the side of the chimney. Then we'd eat it after we had our dinner and got the dishes washed. We'd peel it with a knife and cut it in sections about mouth size and eat it. Oh, it used to be so sweet and good! I have eaten two or three stalks of sugar cane.

And we'd have simmons and bullaces. The bullaces would be gettin ripe around cotton pickin time. They'd be smellin good, but you'd have to go in the woods to get them—they'd be on the vine. We'd be in the field, and which way we'd get the scent of a bullace, we'd hunt the vine. We'd go in the woods and we'd get them—if my father wasn't around.

And in the fall we'd pull peanuts and we'd have those parched peanuts for our extra snack. Or either, livin in the country, we parched corn, but not pop corn, just plain old field corn. You shell it off the cob into the fry pan and heat it up and just keep shakin it till it's brown. It's got a good taste to it. I loved parched corn—I even love it now. And

I remember my father said we'd eat too much corn, so my sister Myrtle would steal the fryin pan, and we would get ears of corn from the crib, and we'd take it down in the woods and cook it anyway. We'd put this pan on a rock and we'd build a fire under it. Then we'd shell this corn and put it in the pan, and we'd sit there until it browned, and we'd eat the corn. We used to eat all we wanted and then bring the pan back and slip it in the kitchen. Oh, boy! We used to be somethin when I was a kid. That's awful! But you know, there's something in all kids' life that they slip and do. Now if that was the baddest thing that we slipped and did, it wasn't too bad after all.

So my father'd give my mother all that scrap cotton for the new mattresses and fresh pillows and quilts for our beds, but the biggest thing we'd look really forward to was the good time out of the seed money what came from the scrap cotton. My father would sell the seeds and he would buy a hoop of *greasy cheese* and *crackers* and *sardines* and *light bread*. You know, my father would be showing us off for doin the work in the summer, I guess. But that was a real good time, and we'd have that.

And after we done picked all the cotton, we'd come home from school in the evenins and my father might kill a pig. He might kill a calf, and my father pickled that, but he never killed a hog in the summer because it would spoil. And he would kill a whole bunch of hogs once a year around Christmas time—sometime he'd kill around eight or nine hogs and smoke the meat in the smokehouse. But he would kill a little pig in the fall and we'd have "fresh meat," we'd call. It'd be cold weather then and it wouldn't spoil like in the summer, and we'd soon eat it up because we had a big family. And whenever my father did kill a hog to have this fresh meat, he'd send the neighbors what they'd call "mess-a-meat" cause when they do kill, they send us some. That's the way it went. But one time he was gonna kill a little pig, and this time he wasn't gonna send any. He told me not to tell it, but the minute I saw my brother comin I went to hollerin, "Davey, come on! We's fixin to kill a hog!" And so my father beat me about it because he didn't want the neighbors to know it.

Oh, I used to tell things. If I knew anything, I would tell it. My brother—we'd do things together and he'd say, "Now don't you tell it." But I'd sho tell it—just sound good to tell it! I figured if I told it I wasn't goin get no whippin nohow. But sometime wind up both of us gettin it and he'd tell me, say, "You see, if you hadn't said nothin, you wouldn'ta got that whippin." And I say, "I don't care." But I did.

I remember another time my father give me a good little lickin—after you kill hogs you make cracklins in the washpot. So one day my father was sittin out there makin cracklins, and he used snuff. He kept it in our little room closet—he always kept his snuff box in there. Well, he was usin it—I wanted to see what it was like. So they was out there makin the cracklins, and while they'se makin the cracklins I say, "I'm gonna get me some of that snuff and put it in my mouth and see." I got a little bit and put it in my lip and I went outside where they were—had forgot I had it in there. I went outside and I spit on the ground, and I just took my foot and covered it over with sand. I didn't know he was watchin me. My daddy said, "Daught?" I says, "Yes, Sir!" "What you got in your mouth?" I said, "Nothin." Swallowed it. I didn't know he could smell it, you know. He said, "*Daught,* what you got in your mouth?"

I said, "Nothin in my mouth." He said, "Come here." And I went there and he looked in my mouth—I done swallowed it, but I had done had snuff in my mouth. He say, "Well," he say, "I ain't goin to whip you cause you had it in your mouth," he say, "but I'm givin you a lickin for lyin." So he beat me because I lied. And so then he went to teachin us, "Tell the truth. Regardless of whatever it is or whatever it costs, tell the truth." Because he always said truth would stand out further than a lie because if you tell *one* lie, you always got to tell *another* lie to cover *that* lie up. See what I mean? You just keep on lyin. But if you tell the truth, the truth'll stand for itself—that's as far as you can go is the truth. And I know he used to say:

> Boys, at all time, tell the truth;
> Let no lie defile your mouth.
> If thou art wrong, be still the same;
> Speak the truth, and bear the blame.
> Truth is honest, truth is sure,
> Truth is sure and must endure.
> Truth is steadfast, sure, and grand,
> Certainly to prevail at last.

My father used to tell us that all the time, so I learned that truth is better than lyin, but I would tell a story in a minute if it got on me too tight. And I got some whippins—I've got a lot of em which I guess I needed. Sometime my father'd put me across his knee, and sometime he'd put my head between his legs. He sometime whipped me with a paddler, sometime with a belt, and sometime with a peach tree switch. Those peach tree switches left welts, and I would holler and holler until he would just tell me to "holler, holler, holler." You know, when somebody tell you to hush, you holler, but when they go to say,

"Holler," then you gonna hush. Then I would hush, and I'd have to nurse my wounds because I had a lot of welts on me when he finished. But time when he was whippin me with the peach tree switch, he'd have me standin off from him, and I'd be dancin aroun and runnin. But I dare not to leave the room—not go outside! Yes, I'd be dancing from that whip and you would, too! You don't want that lick be goin the same place.

Yup, I have got em! And oh, I'd get so mad! I sure did! I thought my father was the most meanest person in the world. He was always on me, but he had a need to be because I had a lotta energy and I talked a lots and I always had a word to say back. So I realize I was wrong now, and I have really thanked him ever since for bringing me up the way he did. He was a wonderful, *wonderful* man.

So in the wintertime we had to eat meat from our own hogs that we killed, we would have dried peas all the winter cause we'd be done harvest them in the fall, we'd have dried butter beans, and we'd have sweet potatoes and white potatoes that we raised. And then we'd have greens still in the garden—collard greens—they stood up and they'd be in there till the next year. And my mother canned tomatoes, she would can corn and okrie, and we'd have syrup which we made. So we had plenty. When the end of the year come sometime we'd get slim—everybody I guess did. But we had *lots* when we *had* lots and it was good—we enjoyed it.

We had a great long table in the little dining room, and that's where we ate. The table was made from boards— my father made it—and we had just plain old chairs what he put bottoms in. When we get ready to eat, say, "Come on, everybody's ready to eat. Come on, you all." We come in and we'd get the dishes outa the safe, and we'd put the dishes and the bowls on the table. Then we all sit down. My father be at the head of the table, my mother be at the side, and then we'll be all around the table. And my father always said grace, and then we'd go to eatin. Everybody's, "Pass me this, pass me that, pass me, pass me." It was good times at mealtimes cause my mother would cook a whole lot, but if it's something that done happened that wasn't workin out too well, my father would talk about it at the table, and then everybody go to fallin away from the table *fast*.

When I was little we'd sit around the fire after supper, and I used to sit on my father's lap all the time and ride his knee as a horse. Davey was older and he thought he was more grown up, I guess, so he didn't do it, but I did it all the time. Then my father used to tell us stories about the little red hen and the little old pig that wouldn't get over the stile. You know that story. And he used to sing little songs—sometime I'd be so sleepy. And I remember my father used to tell us a little poem:

> The bird with the yellow bill
> Hopped up on my window sill,
> Cocked his shiny eyes and said,
> "Aren't you ashamed, you sleepy head!"

He'd say that when it'd be time to go to bed and we're tryin to stay up, or either we were sleepy and didn't want to get up in the morning.

But when we was small and goin to school, my father used to carry me over my lessons right after supper cause he was interested to see what I was learnin. He used to go over my lessons with me all the time. So when I was learnin my ABCs, my father would tell me, "Go over these ABCs with me." He'd take me over em, and then I could go over em all right. And when he started me back over em he said, "What is this?" "E." It'd be a G or maybe somethin else. I didn't know what it was because I would forget it no sooner than he'd get through tellin me cause I just wasn't down at it, you know. And he'd tell me, "If you wasn't so playful and listen to me, you would learn somethin." Then he'd tell me somethin, and if I come back over it the second time and didn't know it, he'd give me a slap. It'd upset me and I couldn't see then because I'd be cryin—my eyes would be fulla tears. And so he let me know that he was intendin me to learn them ABCs by givin me a slap. Now you didn't learn your ABCs like that and you would say, "Well, that seem horrid." Why, he wasn't harsh to me, but he knew that if he didn't get down on me, I wouldn't do it. And I'd know if I was gonna get a lickin, I was gonna do it. I could have learned a whole lot, but I never did take anything to heart. It's no fault of my father's cause he was interested in me, but I didn't take much interest in myself. That was me.

We didn't stay up long after supper—you know, we went to bed early. When you get ready to go to bed, you hang your things on a chair and you put on your sleeping clothes which was outing nightgowns with long sleeves—my mother would be done made them. And when you get your sleeping clothes on, you fall down on your knees by your bed and you say your prayers, run, hop into bed, and get under the covers. The reason why we'd be running because it'd be just as *cold* in them bedrooms. We had a fireplace in our room, but the only thing about it, the heat didn't go no higher than your legs. You'd burn up in front, and then your back would freeze cause no heat was

goin in the room. Everything was goin up the chimney.
Now the houses is warm all over, but then it's cold in the
house. But, anyway, I always turned my back to that fire
and get myself real hot and then hop into bed—say "Good
night, everybody" and hop into bed. Then sometime we'd
talk and rassle around cause there was three of us in one
bed, you know. And we'd be call ourself talking about our
boyfriends. Ain't got no boyfriends, but you know how
you do when you young and you go to school—you think
somebody thinkin about you, or you'd talk about what
somebody done at school. So sometime we'd talk, then
we'd go to sleep.

# TEN

<><><><><><><><><><>

# *Oh, We'd Have Good Plays*

IT WOULD BE dark in the winter when you get up in the morning, so we had to light the lamp. See, they have 'lectric lights now, but lamplight and the fireplace light is the only light that we had at that time. We'd have a lamp with a globe on it and coal oil in it, and we'd have one in each room. We'd burn em so often they get smoked, so we'd have to wash those globes—we'd have to wash em with soap and rinse em and dry em off and shine em up. Then they'd *really* be shinin—they'd throw out *good* light. But Rhoda would get up and light the lamp—the mantlepiece where they sit it in our room—and we'd get up and wash up and we'd get going from there. You could see one look like goin this way and one goin that way. We had to hurry up and get ready and get to school by eight o'clock, so it wasn't no play.

Some mornins before goin to school we had to go to the well—that was before the well went bad. And we'd draw water—not every mornin, but when my mother's gonna wash—and bring it to the house and fill the washpot fulla water and fill all the tubs. And we used to have barrels that would sit at the eaves of the house—when it'd rain they'd catch water. We'd fill them barrels and things fulla water cause she's gonna wash and we's goin to school.

Well, we'd be late probably *that* morning, but not often was we late. And if *we* had to wash, we'd sometimes stay home in the mornin and wash the clothes and hang em up and then go to school after noon. But we made it—we went. We didn't play hooky—we *never* played hooky. We's glad to go to school!

So we'd be comin through those woods in the mornin and oh, boy, we'd be goin to school! And my brother would run off and leave us. One mornin he was hurryin so fast he slipped and fell and wasted his lunch. His lunch was a big old hunk of cornbread and some hunks of white butter and syrup. His butter and his cornbread was layin there, and we come by and we saw it. He done gone on—he didn't have no lunch that day. Now the kids don't want this or that in their lunch. But we's livin on the farm, so for our lunch we had this cornbread or biscuit and butter and cane syrup which soaked in the bread and turned the bread dark by lunchtime. We'd put this lunch in a little tin bucket with a lid on it and get a small fruit jar of milk and take that to school for lunch. I liked it and I ate it. And sometime I have carried a baked sweet potato and a jar of buttermilk—I went to school with that and that was good. But it goes on to show you that we have come a long ways, and a person that have been in my shoes and lived like I lived can appreciate things. Don't you think so?

But when I was at school, my mother's sister Lydia— she was older than I was but we all went to the same school—she would tell me, "I'm going to town," and she would ask my mother to let me go with her. See, my mother wouldn't be sendin *me* to town, but Aunt Georgia would be sendin her daughter Lydia to town for somethin she wanted, and Lydia knowed my mother would let me go with her any time. So she would tell me when she's goin and then she'd tell me, "Now what you do, you steal you a hen or two and a couple dozen eggs, and we'll go downtown because we're gonna sell this." So I'd collect me quite a few eggs from the hen nests—my father made hen nests where the hen would lay her egg. And I put those eggs in a bag and I would take em down the little trail goin through the pasture and on up through by the Buck Harrison's house, and I'd stash those eggs around under the bushes near to the little branch what was down there where I had to cross. Sometime I'd have two or three dozen eggs because I'd be savin em all week. So I'd have the eggs already stole and stashed out, and I could catch the chicken when I leave the house. You know how you do that. And when you get the chicken, you put the chicken in the curb until, if you gonna take two, you get those two. When you get them, then you take em down that trail the way I'm goin to town, and I would tie a string to the chicken leg and tie these chickens to a bush. Then we'd go to town and we took em to the store and they'd buy em. Get maybe fifteen or twenty cent for a chicken and ten cent for a dozen eggs. And when we'd get through sellin what we had, then we'd buy it up in a piece of cheese and sardines and a box of cookies and some lemon drops, and we'd have to eat that up before we got home!

It was common food, but I had plenty to eat, so I didn't have to steal. But Lydia would tell me what to do, and I would do what she tell me. She had me really started on the wrong track—she had me stealin from my mother's house. But I'm goin tell you what broke me up from stealin—she stole thirty-five dollars off the teacher's desk, and thirty-five dollars in that time meant a whole lot, you know. So the principal had her up—they had a big thing of it until her father paid that money back. But that was a scar on her because she had stole it, and seeing her stealing thirty-five dollars broke me up from stealing. I had been stealing those chickens and eggs—I did that a couple of times—but I hadn't got caught. So I come clean before I got caught. And I'm so glad I stopped in time cause if it hadn't broke me up then, I might have been a rogue or something.

But when I used to go to school, I was real fast. I used to *talk* fast and *walk* fast and I *was* fast when I was comin up. I always had big legs, big at the top and come down little like a lamp chimney. They had shape and style! And we used to wear socks come up to your knee, and then they have this top that just fold over, and that top had little workin around it. It was pretty. My father used to get em for us from Sears Roebuck. Sometime they be white, or either they're blue with different kinda tops. They were beautiful. So I had big legs which was popular in my days, and I used to have a real neat waist, and when I walked, I walked fast and I popped my dress tail. And Aunt Nina would say to her daughter, "Why don't you walk like Sara and pop your dress tail like her?" I didn't know I was poppin no dress tail—I would just be walkin. But that's my mother's sister said that, so I'm sure mine was poppin. And I was always told I had a beautiful set of teeth. People would tell me, "Oh," say, "I do love to see you smile," say, "you got the prettiest teeth." So I thought I was lookin all right at that time, I guess.

But, anyway, I wasn't interested much in goin to school—I was fast, as I said. But I didn't do nothin wrong— I didn't do nothin wrong, really. But I'm sure some of the older girls did because I know there was Carrie Ann, she come up with a baby, and then Lucinda—she lives in Philadelphia now—but she had one, too. And who else had one? Willa Jamison, she had a baby. These was girls that were goin to school and had babies. But then they didn't go to school anymore either because they done "broke their legs," they would say, and they wasn't fit to be with in the eyes of the older peoples. Here you can go to school if you have a baby, but there you didn't because girls that never had babies or didn't do these things, they didn't associate with that kind of girl. If she was married it was okay, but if a single girl have a baby, well, we wouldn't be caught with a girl like that. It's against the Bible principle to have children out of wedlock. My mother and father taught us that, and that was it.

But I would be flirtin around at the school because I thought I was somebody. I wasn't because I didn't know nothin and I really shoulda been studying and learnin more. But instead of me learnin what I was supposed to have been learnin, I was always writin little notes to the one I married—we'd be sendin notes to and fro through school. When he's writin a note to me he would say, "The road is wide, and I cannot step it. I love you, Baby. I cannot help it." And, "As the vine grow round the pine, Baby, I want you to be mine." I remember one time I was writin a letter, and I don't know where I got this from, but I had said, "Dear Jesse, I received your lovin epistle today." And I didn't know what "epistle" was, honestly. But, you know, that meant I had received his letter. Professor Sanders got a chance to catch that note I was passin and he asked me what that "lovin epistle" was. I didn't know. So he explained to me what it was and he give me a good old whippin that day about that. Oh, I used to be a *devil* when I was in school, and wouldn't we get a whippin with long switches! You stand out in front of him and swish, shwow! He used to whip us, Professor Sanders. But I wished he hadda kept on whippin me—I wouldn'ta gotten married to this guy.

Professor Sanders always wanted us to learn, and he would tell my father that we had a good ability if we'd just get into it. But I didn't wanta settle down to learnin, and I didn't. I could learn any yells, poems, anything like that. I used to be a cheerleader and I was always wantin to be out practicin our yells. Mrs. Holly would tell us these yells and learn em to us, and then Professor Sanders would tell us what we could say and what we couldn't. I remember one day—Professor Sanders had done forbid us to say one cheer because it had some "damn" in it: Damn it to hell, we love it so well. . . . So I was out there sayin,

> Rickety, rackety, rust to rust,
> I promise not to cuss, to cuss, to cuss.
> But damn it to hell,
> I love it so well,
> I must cuss or bust.

Professor Sanders was somewhere around and he heard me and he said, "Get me on in there." He give me a few licks for that. He did! But we'd have ball games against different schools and I'd get out there and I would be yellin. I used to have a good time! And our uniform what we had on was really beautiful. We wore white midis with collars and we had black ties, we had black bloomers pleated all the way to the knee, then we had long socks and white tennis shoes. I guess the officials of the school must have got em all for us cause they all was just alike. And oh, boy!

I'd be yellin! Come home, I'd be so hoarse, but I used to lead them. I got a lot outa life when I was young! I just wish I could live my life over again.

So instead of learnin, that's what I was doin. And I always liked to be in every program that they had at school. We'd have a Thanksgiving program, a Christmas program, and a program at the end of school. I was in them because I always loved poems—I liked the rhyme—so I could learn them. My father didn't have to hit me—not one time—when I was learnin those poems because that was somethin I wanted to do. And I could *act!* I could act in different plays that other kids was so bashful and couldn't learn things that I could. So anything that they wanted to come out pretty good at school, they'd give me a book to learn it from. That's the truth—the professor would do it, so I learned em.

When I was in about the tenth grade I recited "'Lias, 'Lias, Bless de Lord." That's one of the things I used to recite. It was like a play, but it wasn't nobody but 'Lias and me—just the two of us—and he was doin what I told him to do. I say,

> 'Lias! 'Lias! Bless de Lord!
> Don't you know this day abroad?
> If you don't get up from there, you scamp,
> There's gonna be trouble in dis camp.
> You think I goin let you sleep
> While I make your board and keep?
> Huh! That's a pretty howdy-do—
> Don't you hear me, 'Lias, you?
> If I come marchin cross that floor
> You ain't goin have no time to snore.
> Daylight's all a-shinin in
> And you layin up there asleep—now that's a sin!
> You march yourself and wash your face,

> And don't you splatter all over this place!
> Take this comb and comb your head—
> It looks just like a featherbed.

When we went to the table, I say,

> Sit down at dat table there;
> Just you whimper if you dare!
> Fold your arms and bow your head,
> And you wait until de blessin's said.

And then when we start blessin the table, I said,

> "Lord have mercy upon our soul . . ."

And while we got our eyes closed, he'd be reachin for a roll. I say,

> Don't you dare catch de rolls!

And I said,

> "Bless this food we gwine to eat."

I say,

> Sit still, 'Lias! I hear your feet.
> You just try that trick again.
> "Givin joy. Thanks. Amen!"

Oh, we'd have good plays! And my father and my mother would be there—they would come and listen. I think all kids liked for their parents to listen—you feel look like you got some support when your parents is around. I felt that way—they cared, you know what I mean? But one time the professor had given me another poem and they didn't want me to recite it. It was in the book and they heard me say it, but they didn't want me to recite it because, you see, they knew what it was all about and they thought that the white peoples might dislike it, I guess, and they

didn't want no outcome to be on me. I remember this poem
well:

> I've done stayed silent long enough
> And tried to hold my jaws,
> But I must say a word or so
> About these Jim Crow Laws.
> God made us all from white to black
> And made us in one mold,
> And then He breathed us all to life
> The breath that made the soul.
> He gave us just one kind of day
> And just one kind of night,
> And that's enough to prove to all
> This Jim Crow Law ain't right.

Then it says,

> We milk the cows,
> We strain the milk,
> We cook their cakes and pies.
> Our hand mix up the bread they eat,
> And that is no surprise.
> We take their babies in our arms;
> We hug and kiss and bite.
> They make us face that Jim Crow Law
> And tell us that it's right.
> And when some big thing come to town
> They'll put us in the back,
> And on the train we'll ride ahead
> To catch what's on the track.
> They'll mix us up with baggage, too,
> And everything in sight,
> And make us pay first-class fare
> And pretend that that is right.
> But to prove yourself a man
> Is to vote and judge the law,
> And come along this world can see
> This Jim Crow Law ain't right.

But when we would have a program, Professor Sanders would invite white peoples and he would reserve seats

for the white peoples to sit in the front rows. So they'd be there—they were some of the peoples that had stores in town and their families. But do you know, I didn't know a lotta those white folks cause we wasn't around no white folks that much. We didn't live next door to em cause we was back over in those woods—closest we lived was to Mr. Garrett, and we just worked for him every once in awhile. And whenever we see any of the other white peoples, we'd go down to the little town cause that's where they were livin. But you didn't see no white people walkin around downtown cause there wasn't but about three stores and a post office down there. And when we went to town, we didn't hang around, because my father told us, "You go into town, you tend to your own business, you turn right around and come back home." So he didn't say why, but that's what we did.

But I never did see any trouble in town, and we never was bothered by no white peoples really. We didn't bother them and they didn't bother us. One of em had done kicked my son Jerome once, and I didn't like that. But that's one thing I can say that *we* didn't really come up hard like a lotta peoples did under the white peoples. And my father never taught us against the white peoples and he never taught us that the white peoples were better than we were. It would make you believe that a white person must be better because they had nice homes comparable to what we had, and they'd have on little print dresses or a shirt and a pair of pants. And, too, we had the feelin that they didn't wanta be around us because we couldn't go in their school and if we went downtown, it was so far you could go and so far you didn't. But we didn't say nothin to each other about it—we didn't—and my father never talked to us about white people. No, he didn't do it. So really I didn't have nothin to say against the white peoples because they never did nothin to us personally. If they did anything to us, it was somethin they did out there and we didn't know nothin about it. And so long as you don't know nothin about a thing, it don't worry you nohow.

But I was always on stage, so I often wondered why did *they* have to have the front seats? But every time we'd have a program, they'd be there—until the time when I said that poem about the Jim Crow Law. I don't think they liked that poem because the white people didn't come no more after that. The white peoples didn't come no more because it said that this Jim Crow Law ain't right. Now see, that's plain as the nose on the face. So the white peoples were thinkin no doubt that we was learnin that we all are the same—made just alike and everything—only one got one color and one's another. And they didn't want us to learn it because when Martin Luther King wanted everybody to eat in the same restaurant and go to the same toilet, you see what they did to him—they kilt him. But he opened it up much plainer to everybody that you just as good as anybody else. I may not have as much as you, I may not have the education you got, but still, if I conduct myself as a decent person, I'm just as good as anybody. I learnt this when I learnt this poem. That's the way I feel, and I don't care who it is—I don't care if it's the president—I would tell him the same thing. I would.

I went to school until the eleventh grade—I went to school up until I was married. In the mornin we had devotional. We had a piano player and he'd be "Dumba, dumba, dumba, dumba, dumba, dumba. . . ." We'd be marchin two by two, comin in and takin our seats. Oh, I'd be struttin, and you could hear my voice higher than anybody else's. I would sing loud and clear! I'm tellin you, that's the truth! But we'd march every mornin in there and we'd sing. And when we get through singin, Professor Sanders would pray, and then he would always teach us things and he'd tell us how to stand up for ourselves. He always said, "You can be somebody"—that's what he would say. "You study your books, you get an education, you can go to college, you can be somebody." But at that time I didn't really care because I didn't wanta go to school. What I was gonna do, I was gonna go to school till I got old enough not to go, and then I was gonna get married. But Professor Sanders would tell us things, and then we'd march out to our classrooms. Then we had our mornin sessions which was arithmetic first, and we'd have geography, and we would have English. In the evenin, we'd have home economics, and we'd have spelling. Then three-thirty, we'd be ready to go home.

We'd come along from school with other children like Armetta Tucker, Emmy Lou Randolph, Lizzie Randolph, and the Cunninghams and Creola Randolph. We'd come straight home—we didn't go to nobody's house. But you know how kids do—they stop and they talk in the forks of the road when they departin. But when we got where everybody done turned off from us and wasn't nobody else there but us, then we'd go straight home. We'd pull off our school clothes and we'd eat sweet potatoes and go get this lightwood. We didn't do it every day—we did it every so often in the wintertime. We used to have a box for the lightwood sittin at the fireplace—we put it in there. And, too, we'd milk the cows. When we do all that, then we'd eat because it'd be about night then and everybody be home.

When we finished supper, *we* had to wash the dishes before *we* went in the house for good at night. We didn't have no sink, but we had a dishpan, and we had this reservoir on our stove and it always would keep water hot, so we didn't have no trouble havin to wash the dishes. We just had ordinary dishes and we had some glasses—we had some pretty glasses—but we didn't use em till the company come cause we used mostly salmon cups to drink out of. My father would sometime buy salmons in the can and sardines in the can. Oh, boy! Sardines was a treat, and crackers—"salty crackers," we'd call. But that's the only two canned things we'd buy because my mother always did her own canning, you know. So you take the salmon cans and cut em off real nice and smooth and you can wash em out—you'd have those salmon cups. We used them for milk. They was nice to drink out of.

But we had a night apiece to wash the dishes, and if I wash the dishes tonight, you wash them the next night. We rotated it so nobody didn't do it all. But whoever washed the dishes, the others stayed in the kitchen with her because one wash, another dry, and another puttin em up in the safe—that is, if Rhoda wasn't asleep. Rhoda would go to sleep, and when she went to sleep, well, we'd put salt and pepper or bakin soda in her mouth. Then we'd go out of the kitchen and leave her in the dark. Oh, boy!

And I used to scald the hogs from the kitchen. They would go under the kitchen at night and squeal if it's cold weather—you know, one tryin to get closer to another one. And it was just a board floor, so you could see a hog through the cracks between these plank boards if he came under the house, so I'd get me some water outa the reservoir and just pour it down through there, and boy, they'd come out from under there with their tails in the air! And my father say, "What's wrong with them hogs? What's wrong with them hogs?" I wouldn't know, but old Rhoda holler, "Sister done scald the hogs!" So my father found out I was scaldin em. Oh! That's the meanest thing I used to do— I used to be mean in that way! But after my father found out that I was doin these things, well, he didn't have to whip me but *once* and I didn't do it. But I *wished* to.

So we had to wash the dishes in the evenin. Then we'd go right out of the kitchen, on the porch, and right in the house in Momma and them's room. We mostly gathered by the fire in Momma and them's room because we just liked to be around them. We studied our lessons for the next day, and my father would sit down and he would do things like fix our shoes. When we got tore up shoes and heels off em, my father would try to fix them the best he could. He'd take a patch and put it on them shoes. He'd use a big sewin needle and an awl—punch holes with the awl—and he'd use beeswax to do the threads and he'd sew em. Or he'd put em on the shoe last and half sole our shoes. My father used to do that himself. And I remember my father would polish his shoes. He'd take smut from the chimney—smut from the chimney be black. He'd mix it up with some water and put it on the shoe with a rag and let it dry and when it get dry, then he'd take somethin like a wool cloth and he'd just *shine* his shoes. He'd brighten em up for Sunday.

But when Momma and them be gone to bed, we'd fix our hair for the next morning. We'd steal my father's curry comb what you do a horse, and we'd get us lard outa the lard bucket and grease our hair. Then we'd take this curry comb and pull our hair and have it slick through. Or either we'd take a fork—some forks got four prongs—we'd take that fork and we'd heat it in the fireplace and we'd go through our hair with that fork. When we started usin it, we wouldn't take it back to the table—we'd keep that fork hid for our use. But when we were smaller, my grandmother used to wrap our hair. She used to ravel out old stockings, and then she would part off our hair and wrap all the hair and tie it back. But when we were older and we thought we was lookin at the boys and everything, we didn't wrap our hair then. We'd straighten it with the curry comb or the fork.

When we were ready for school the next day we'd go to bed, and I would hurry and get into bed first in order that I wouldn't have to blow the lamp out because whoever blow out the lamp, she gotta come to bed in the dark. So Rhoda or Molly had to blow the light out till they'd ask, "Who gonna blow out the lamp tonight?" And then it come to where I had to do it, too. We each had to do it, same as washing dishes.

So everybody go to bed. But in the wintertime we had to get up at night and sometime put more wood on the fire to keep the house warm. If I did it tonight, you do it tomorrow night, and you do it the next night. Oh, boy! I'm tellin you! And you have to use the chamber in the house at night. You know, we didn't have no toilet—you had to go outside. But you didn't go out there every time you wanted to get up, dark as it is at night, so we'd go out before we went to bed. One of the little ones say, "I have to go out." "Me, too." Well, probably all of us would go out and just get some cotton leaves if it's cotton time. You see, we used to order from Sears and Roebuck and they'd

send you a catalogue. We put it in the privilege, and when
that ran out, we'd use leaves—cotton leaves and sweet gum
leaves—and corn husks. It's true. But we'd have to use the
chamber with a lid on it at night, and I empty it this morning, you empty it tomorrow morning.

   Oh brother! We have lived! I don't know how we sur-
vived, but it didn't seem bad then. You see, everybody
was livin in that way when we were down there and nobody
didn't think anything about it because that's all we knew.
We didn't know no other place—and some still livin that
way now.

◇◇◇◇◇◇◇◇◇

# ELEVEN

# Christmas Gif', Hand It Here

W E JUST came up real common—that was the way we came up. And we used to work hard—we used to put all we had in whatever we did. I think my father appreciated it, and in return he used to do things to uplift us—he would try to make us happy doin things that he thought we would like. And so my father had the house painted. It wasn't painted always, but as we was growin on up into ladyhood and we'd have a little company, my father had the house painted outside to look nice. It was painted white trimmed in green, and we did like it cause not many peoples around had their houses painted. That was special.

But we was *far* from being well off. The inside of the house was just boards, plain boards—the walls and the ceiling. And when Christmas come, that's the only time we'd decorate. We'd buy colored papers and make chains. We'd take the scissors and we'd cut this paper in strips and go in the kitchen and get some flour and make a paste, and we'd paste em together and make chains. Then we'd put em up across the ceiling from one corner to the next— we'd go this way and that way—and then we'd hang a big red Christmas bell in the middle.

We didn't buy our Christmas tree—me and Rhoda and

Molly would go in the woods and cut it. The Christmas tree that we used to get, we used to call cedar trees. We'd cut one down and we'd bring it on in Christmas Eve night and we put it in the corner of the company room. We didn't have any 'lectric lights at that time, but we'd make these chains, and we'd have them all over the Christmas tree. And we put smilax vines on the tree—they were vines that grew on bushes. We'd go in the woods and get smilax vines and we'd put em across the door. And we'd get mistletoes and we'd tie em in bunches and hang em up in the house. And, too, we used to get holly. They'd have little berries all on em and we'd break em off and we'd take little bunches and tie em together and hang them up, too. It would be pretty. So that would be our decoration—that's all we had then.

We never got presents all through the year like some kids now get somethin all the time. We had only one time that we got something—that was Christmas. Then we'd get presents like nuts and candies and fruit. We wouldn't know what an apple was from one *Christmas* until another. We had apples on the tree, but we consider them as just any old apple. But to have a Delicious apple at Christmas time, you could smell it! And bananas and oranges—they smelled so *good*. My father would hide em in the smokehouse and say, "Santy Claus will be comin such and such a time." Then our things would be by the fireplace as if Santy Claus came down the chimney and left em there.

One Christmas morning when I was quite small I had two oranges, I had two apples, and I had a thing called a comeback—you roll it and it'll come back to you. You've seen those—I had one of those in my Christmas stocking. I had two apples and two oranges, and I had some raisins on the stems, and I had this comeback. And then I had this boy doll with rompers—he had a pretty face and he had on a cap—I had this doll sittin there. *And* I had a pair of shoes in a box. So I admired everything, and when I got to the shoes, I stashed them in the fire. Those were some new shoes that my father bought me to enrichen my Christmas, but I didn't want the shoes because I had gone barefeeted so *long* and so *much*, shoes wasn't interestin to me. I wasn't interested in nothin but the little boy doll and some fruit and candy. So I did it! My brother hollered— cause he called me "Girlie"—"Oh, Pa! Girlie done throwed those shoes in the fire!" So I got a good whippin on Christmas morning.

But my mother would cook up for Christmas—she'd have boxes of cakes and pies—and we'd eat all day long. And then that's the time when peoples'll really visit you. Sometime it'd be my mother's people—Aunt Georgia and some of them, or Aunt Nina, some of those peoples—or just most anybody that would know em probably come by. So when you'd see somebody comin you'd say, "Christmas gif', hand it here," and they'd give you a coin or somethin, and then you go cut em a pie or cake and fix em a big plate and they sit down and eat. And probably you give em some fruit or candy when they get ready to leave, and then they go on to somebody else's house. So that's how we'd celebrate Christmas. That was some time!

I enjoyed Christmas up until I was about ten, and my brother broke that up by tellin me there wasn't no Santy Claus. Then he says, "I know where the stuff is and you come and I'll show it to you." And he showed it to me—it was in the smokehouse—and so then Christmas was over.

After we learned that my father was the Santy Claus,

he'd buy the presents and bring them home, and on Christmas Eve night, after the smaller ones that were still thinking it was Santy Claus had gone to bed, he would divide everything out equal. "This is yours, and this is yours. This is yours, and that's yours"—just like that. When he got through dividin out what he was gonna give *us* for Christmas, he went outside—he always walked outside at night. And so when he got outside he said that was his mother sittin out there on a stump. Say, "I reckon Momma come for her Christmas, too." Now he told us that—he said he saw her! That was the first year that she had been dead.

I was about fifteen years old when my grandmother died because she died in December 1926. She was old, and she had got to where she went to wanderin away from home, and she'd get lost. My father would look for her and he would bring her home. Rhoda took care of my grandmother when she started runnin away. She used to get out there in the yard, she'd look up, she'd say, "Oh, I'm goin *home,* you all, cause I can hear my chickens crowin over yonder. They hungry, and I got to go home and feed em."

If somebody's goin to die, the death owl come to the house and cries, "Ha, ha, ha, ha, ha, ha, ha." They go so *lonesome*—they *real* lonely. And they'd say that it was a sign of death, so you'd tie a knot in your sheet and say that would choke him and he won't quiver. All them old signs, they don't pay them things no attention no more. But whenever this owl be shiverin, my mother's goin to tie a knot in the sheet—she'd choke it so he'd stop sayin that. So the night before my grandmother died, this owl came up on the porch and was shiverin—sure did! Nobody couldn't sleep for that bird—so she did die.

My grandmother died about nine o'clock one morning, and one of my sisters, Essie, was born about eight o'clock that same morning in that same house. I ain't never been there when the baby was born—we always stayed at my mother's sister's house. They lived up there not too far from us, and we were glad to go somewhere to spend the night cause we never went no place to spend the night. And they wouldn't tell us where the baby came from— they would tell us that the baby came from over behind the Blue Mountain or that the baby came out of a stump. I don't know how come we couldn't see she got fat and got small—that's what we shoulda been lookin at. Maybe Rhoda and them did, but I didn't have that thought at all.

So Aunt Ruth was at our house because her mother was sick. It sound like she needed our room, so they let us go to Aunt Nina's to spend the night. When we come back the next mornin this baby was there, and Gramma died a little after that. Cause when we come back it was time for breakfast, so we went in the dining room, and when we come back in the house Aunt Ruth says, "Well, Momma slipped away from us while you was in the kitchen." My mother was in the other room—the baby was born just a few minutes before. So one went out, and one came in that same day.

# TWELVE

# You May Plow Here

THE DOGWOOD would be bloomin everywhere when springtime come, and also the honeysuckle would be shootin out their blooms. They smell so good—you could smell the honeysuckle from the woods. And there was a bush called sweet shrub—they grew in the woods and they be smellin real good. Also the jonquils would bloom in the yard, and the bumblebees would be out. That's the time my father and them would start breakin up the land for planting.

My father would start breakin up the land in March. He would be plowing by himself—he'd plow from sunup to sundown—and the only company that he really had was listenin to the birds. Whatever it sound like the birds say, he would put it into words. He was plowing one day at a low place that had been wet and had done growed up with a whole lotta weeds, and a bird was singing when he was plowing, and he made a song from what the bird sung:

> You may plow here
> Just as much as you please.
> You may plow here
> Just as deep as your knees.
> But I will tell you
> Right before your face,

You ain't goin make nothin here
But burrs and weeds,
But burrs and weeds.

That'd mean cockleburs and jimson weeds. What he was plowin, I guess he had a feelin that the bird was tellin him he wasn't gonna make nothin there, so he made that song himself. But it was a great crowd of us, and as the kids grew my father took in more land—he would be extendin the crop by takin in some land which had been laid out so we could make enough to feed all of us.

So when farmin time came, my father would break up the land first. Then when time come to plant the crops, we'd have to stay home some days in order to help get things in line. See, it was four of us—my brother and Molly, Rhoda and me—plus Sally and them, too. They was small but they worked. My father would keep us out of school a half day—maybe two of us today or three today, and maybe two or three the next day. We'd work in the mornin and then go to school at noontime. Or sometime two'd work all day or three'd work all day and then go to school the next day. He wouldn't keep us out day after day—we'd rotate. Then we'd go to school until we finished school, and that was in May.

So we started stayin home from school when time come to make rows in the field and plant. My father got two plows goin then—course he would plow, and Rhoda would help. Davey used to help my daddy plow when he went to school, but he didn't finish high school—he went to workin out. He was workin at a place called Springfield. He was sawin logs and he wasn't makin nothin much, but when he'd make his money he'd bring it home and give it to my father. And when he went to workin out he was

stayin over— he was comin home once a week—so that's
why Rhoda was plowin.

I couldn't plow. I couldn't plow because I couldn't get
along with the mule. An hour or so about all the mule and
me could do because, you know, I always was the type
that was quick. It had to be *now* or either we didn't get
along. See, when I would plow the mule, if I tell the mule
to gee or haw, if that mule didn't, I'd hit that mule, and
then that mule gonna jump, and when he jump, well, I'll
probably take up half of what would be there.

And then, too, we had this horse what my daddy had
me plowin. Her name was Daisy—Old Daisy's the one I
tried to plow. I fussed so and beat on that horse so till
when I get to the end of the row and tried to turn that
horse around, that horse would run at me and kick me.
I'd turn that plow loose and I'd just leave there screamin
cause I was afraid of her. I couldn't get along with no horse
and no mule. Uhn, uhn! I'd fuss too much. Everybody'd
know I was behind the plowstock cause I'd be "Whoa!"
"Gee!" "Haw!" I couldn't do it. I didn't mind goin to field
cause that was our livin. And I would *like* to ride the horse—
we went to field on the horse cause the field was so far
from the house. We'd tie the horse on a rope and let the
horse graze around, and then when we come home, all
three of us be on that horse. So I remember one day we
done come all the way from the field, and when we got
nearby the house, all of em sittin on the porch, and here
we came ridin in. I wanted to show off—decided I'd make
the horse trot. So I took and, unbenounced to the others,
I kicked the horse and the horse jumped and we just went
right off. We didn't have no saddle—my father would use
the saddle whenever he'd go to mill or what not, but just

us goin to field, we didn't have no saddle. We'd ride bare-
back if we didn't throw a sack up there, but most of the
time we barebacked it. So we all slid right off that horse,
right off her. Oh, boy! That's the truth! So I liked to ride
the horses and the mules—we mostly rode the mules to
field because they were tamer—but I never could plow.
Rhoda plowed. She's the easy type—never know she's
there.

Rhoda or my daddy be openin the row, and I'd be puttin out fertilizer. It was somethin called guano—that was
the fertilizer. It would be used in the cotton field and the
cornfield. It would make them yield more. My father used
manure in the garden and in the potato patch—when he
clean up the cow pen and the lot, he'd always pull all the
manure in one corner, and that's what he'd do with that
manure. But you buy the guano in a sack. My father would
get it from the store in town. He'd buy sacks of guano—
he'd have wagonloads. He'd bring some home one day
and then he'd go back another day until he brought it all
home, and the corn would be out of the crib almost, and
he put some in there cause it couldn't get wet.

But the way we was puttin this fertilizer out, you carried it in a sack on your back. And at that time they had
somethin that was called a guano horn that you drop this
fertilizer down through. The top of it was like a funnel,
and it had a long tube to it that the fertilizer run down
through into the row. It was about as long as a broom
handle. You hold the guano horn in one hand, and you
use your other hand to reach into the bag and get a hand
fulla fertilizer and drop it down this horn—it was aimed
down in the row. So you holdin it in your hand, and you'd
be walkin fast—you gotta continue to walk in order that it
didn't pile up in one place. You had to walk fast, and when

that fertilizer give out, you put another handful in and just keep walkin. When you get to the end of the row, you turn right around and do another row. Reachin in the sack and droppin it down this horn—just reachin and goin. Go down one row and come up another and go down another. And then my father or Rhoda would come along behind you and cover it up with the plow. One would be openin the row with a scooter plow, and the other one would bed up the row with a turn plow. That's the way we get the fertilizer in. Now, you know we did a lotta fertilizin—puttin out—didn't we!

Next thing would come the planting. My father would open up the rows in the field and if it's gonna be cotton, you plant cotton, and if it's gonna be corn you drop corn. The corn went in first—in April we would always plant the corn. My father always kept some of the healthy-looking ears of corn for seed, so we'd get these ears of corn from the crib and shell up enough to last all day—sometime we'd shell up enough to last two days—and we put it in a burlap sack. We would carry that sack on the shoulder, or cither if you didn't want to take a sack, you could take a pail, but the sack held more. You had to have enough corn to drop four or five rows. You drop the corn every step—you drop three or four grains in each hill so that if some didn't come up, some would come up.

We'd have to drop the corn, but now when it come to cotton, my daddy had a cotton planter. You put the seeds in this planter—it was pulled by a mule—and it would open the row and sow the seeds. Click, click, click, click—it would be dropping the seeds. Then somebody would cover it up behind, and that would stay there then until the seeds come up.

So everything would be planted accordin to schedule.

But when it was real dry at planting time, my father used to wet the cotton seeds and roll them in the dirt before he planted them. That would cause them to sprout quicker. He never wet all of them, but he would do that in order to help them germinate. But mostly it rains a lot in the spring, and if it had been raining and had everywhere wet for so long, then my father couldn't plow and that would put you behind, so then you would hurry to catch up, and to do that you would just go in and plant the seeds right on top of that fertilizer. You see, after you lay the fertilizer in the row, if it's not ready to plant, somebody covers over the rows, and then when it's ready, it's got to be opened up again and planted and covered over again. But when you're behind, you drop the seed on top of the fertilizer and that would be less work and less time.

When it rained my father'd make us cut the bushes what be done grew up in the fields—they would mostly be sassafras and gum bushes. We'd do that when it's too wet to do anything else—we'd get all those bushes cut down and outa the way and tied up on the edge of the field. Oh, we used to work! We didn't play—we worked! I'm glad to be from it—I've had enough of that. But when spring come, I still have to plant somethin. I'm used to it. Somethin that is really woven into me is that spring planting!

When school was out in May, we'd know we'd have to go to field every day then because it's nice and warm and everything begin to be big enough to get to work at. We'd hill cotton first. The cotton come up so thick, so when it gets about a hand high, my father and Rhoda would bar off the cotton with a turn plow, which mean they would narrow the row. They'd turn the dirt *from* the cotton row on each side so we could chop the cotton—thin it out and get rid of the grass. We'd go in with the hoe and you chop this, you leave that, you chop out that, and you leave this. That's what was leavin the hills of cotton. And Molly always was nearsighted and she'd just as soon leave a weed for a stalk of cotton. My father always would get after her about that, so what happened then, my father let her be the nurse and my mother would come out awhile in the mornings. But you thin the cotton out two or three stalks to a hill, no more. The healthiest ones you leave. So that's the way we do it till we got it all chopped out. And then they'd come back and they would dirt up the cotton with a sweep plow—that is, throw the dirt back up on both sides of the row, hilling up the row and leaving a furrow between the rows. And then it would stay like that until, if it got real grassy, Rhoda and my father would run the middles out with a larger sweep plow, which is run down the furrow left between the rows by the smaller sweep plow, and that'd throw more dirt back to the cotton. This removes the grass. Then one more time we'd probably hoe that cotton. When you thinnin it out, that's choppin the cotton. But the next time you go, you hoein the cotton—that mean you gettin the grass out of it so it can grow. And that's all then until around July it start bloomin, and oh, they were pretty blooms! It looked pretty when the cotton was all bloomed out. But when it start bloomin, well, you don't mess with it then because you'd be knockin the squares off.

So we'd chop cotton until we'd get it all chopped out, and then we'd thin corn—we'd go in the cornfield and thin corn and replant corn. You thin the corn when it get about a half a leg high—not quite to your knees. We'd have to thin it out cause it would be too thick. If you had it too thick the ears wouldn't be as large, so we'd have to dig it out with a hoe. Whether you pull it up or dig it up, it's got to come out by the roots cause if it didn't, it would come up again.

But sometime the corn didn't come up well. If you planted corn and it rained afterwards, the corn would rot in the ground and it didn't come up good—it was missin places. So if it's wet when you thinnin the corn, you can reset it by diggin it up and planting it in the next space that didn't have enough. Or either we'd take two or three ears of corn in a sack, and we always had pockets in our dresses, so we'd shell the corn and we'd put the corn in our pocket, and then where corn was missin and didn't come, we'd go along and dig a hole and drop corn and cover it up and go find another spot that needs corn planted. That's what you call replanting corn. We had to do that on rainy days because it would take root quicker if it was planted when it was wet. But we did that until we got the whole crop finished.

And we'd plant peas between some hills of early corn. Usually we had a pea patch, but we'd have peas growin in the early corn, and then we'd go there and pick peas and get roastin ears all the same time. Then too, we had peas planted in the cotton field around the house—sunflowers and peas in the missing places where the cotton didn't come up too well. And we'd put corn in there, too—we'd plant crib corn in the spaces in the cotton. So one field didn't produce just no one somethin—we'd put lotta different things in the fields.

From the corn and the cotton and the peas, we had to plant the sugar cane and sweet potatoes and peanuts. In the wintertime the cane that wasn't going to be made for syrup was put in a cane bank and you put dirt over that.

You "bank the cane," as you call it, for the winter. And then when it get warm in the spring it start comin up through the dirt, and then you rakes the dirt back off the cane and you open the rows in the field and you lay the cane down with the eyes up, and it'll come up from those eyes. So that's the way we keep cane from the one end of the year to the other.

And then we'd set out potatoes—when it rained we'd set them out. When springtime comes it always was some little potatoes left in the potato bank. You dig a hole and you lay em down and then you cover em over—this bed is called a potato bed. You make the bed usually in a corner of the garden that's already fenced in so the hogs can't get there to eat it up. When it gets warm, the warm rain brings shoots up outa the potatoes, and when they get a little better than past your wrist you can just pull em off. And you have your rows already made up and you've got a stick—you take that stick and dig a hole and set your potato sprout and pat the dirt up to it. When they start growing, you can cut the vines off and set them out—reset them. They grow. We'd keep on settin em until we'd made rows and rows of potatoes!

And we grew our peanuts. We'd eat peanuts all winter until we'd eat down to so many my mother figured we had to save peanuts to plant, so we'd shell these peanuts and she would put em in a sack and put em away. She kept the sack in the little room closet, and I made me a hole in the sack about as big as my finger, and I would get me a few peanuts every so often. I'd eat them—I was *takin em*. But the peanuts would be shelled and we'd carry them in a bucket and we didn't have nothin to do but drop them in the row when they open up the row, and you slip a peanut in your mouth every once in awhile when you be droppin them. They'd be so good! Now that's the way the peanuts started off for the next year.

So we had plenty to do in the springtime—there was always somethin to do. We'd plant the crops and then we'd chop cotton. When we'd get through choppin cotton there was corn to be thinned out, and by the time we'd get around doin corn and peanuts and potatoes and everything, it's time to go back and do that cotton over again. So it was from one field to the other one. We worked hard! We did! But I just loved it! I did! We had fresh air, sunshine, and wide-open spaces. Only time I was ready to leave home when Rhoda got married. Davey married first, then Rhoda's sister got married. After Rhoda's sister got married, it was Rhoda next got married. And I just said I wasn't goin to stay home then because I was the oldest one and I knew all the *big work* was gonna be on me. And I knew that I wasn't gonna get a chance to go anyplace unless I gotta whole tag followin behind me, which woulda been the small kids. I didn't want that because you know how you do when you feel you've growed up—you don't wanta be foolin with the little ones all the time. And so I thought I was lovin this guy, but I didn't love him. And he couldn't never loved me to treat me like he did. So neither one of us did love each other, but I hurried up and I got married after the others did.

# THIRTEEN

# I Had to Learn on My Own

I DIDN'T stay home a year after Rhoda got married because, you see, Molly, Rhoda, and myself married cousins. Molly's husband and my husband's first cousins, and also Rhoda's husband and my husband was first cousins. But Molly's husband wasn't no relation to Rhoda's husband because Rhoda's husband's father and my husband's mother was brother and sister, see? And my husband's father and Molly's husband's mother were brother and sister. They was all cousins, and we's courtin all cousins. And my brother told me, "Girlie," he said, "those old boys you all courtin, they ain't nothin, so why don't you all leave them alone?" Well, you know when anybody go and tell you anything like that, if you would take heed you would do. But it look like you get more determined, don't it? So we just kept on goin with em and my cousins married and I married—we all married. I got married in April and my birthday—that was goin be in December, the twelfth day of December—I was going to be nineteen. So I was eighteen when I got married.

But I wished I hadda stayed home because my father wanted me to go to college. He told me that if I would stay home and finish school, he would send me to college because he had raised his sister's two children—he had did the best that he could do with us all together. So then, and only then, that he had the opportunity to do something for me, bein his *own* child—he could send me to college if I would go. But I didn't know what college even was. We was down in the country just goin to school, come back home and eat, study our lessons. I didn't see nothin that was interestin enough around me to make me want to go to college. The people right around us was doin the same thing that I was doin, see. Now if my father hadda moved from the South and moved North, no doubt I would have gone to school and then to college because it coulda been somethin here woulda interested me and it woulda made me want to go. But we didn't have nobody to learn by and I didn't know that me not goin to school would be hinderin me on down the line.

    So I went to the eleventh grade and stopped. I didn't wanna go—I was too fast. But I never broke his heart in no way. I never had kissed a boy even until the night my husband asked my father, could we get married? Then he kissed me that night. We was in the company room and my father was outside and he saw it. That's one thing— my father wasn't gonna stay in that house while we had company—he always would circle around outside. And the shades had to be up just like they were—you didn't pull no shades down at our house, *no*. So I *knew* that he probably was round somewhere, so I didn't want him to kiss me. But oh, he wanted to kiss me and he just had asked my father for me and we was gonna get married, and he kissed me. So my father didn't say nothin that night. The next mornin we got up and we's havin breakfast and I was reachin over and gettin biscuits cause I always liked biscuits and syrup. I was reachin gettin biscuits and my

father says, "Well, Daught," he says, "you eatin you biscuits this mornin like the way you was kissin Jesse last
night." *Oh*, I'd got enough biscuits right there! But I know
good and well I wasn't kissin him—I just let him kiss me
once. But if I got by with that, that was somethin good!
But I didn't get by. He saw it. He's gonna see what went
on, but that was the only thing went on. We wasn't no
type of bad. We had to be home before sundown. If that
sun was goin down and was gettin red, boy, we'd pull off
our shoes and we would go home cause if we didn't, we
would get a good whipping with a peach tree switch with
prongs on it. So we went, I'm tellin you!

I married on a Sunday in April in nineteen thirty cause
my son Benjamin was born the next year in May. Around
five-thirty the neighborhood peoples started gathering for
the wedding. There was just some of my mother's people
like her sisters and the children of them and us what lived
there. And my sister-in-laws to be and brother-in-laws to
be was there. And the Reverend Randolph, the man that
baptized me when I was eleven years old, he married me.
I got married on my front porch. I married in a powder-
blue dress my sister-in-law Rebecca made for me, and I
stood under an arch. It was made out of a saplin that'd
bend, and it had flowers all on it—my mother and
them dressed it up with white paper flowers. It was big
enough for two to stand under, and that's where we got
married.

After we got married didn't nothin happen that day.
We didn't have no dinner like peoples have now. We just
left. I carried my suitcase—I had a little suitcase with dresses
and underclothes and nightgowns in it. I had dresses what
we always wear on Sundays, I had my shoes, and maybe

I had a pair of stockin—maybe, I said. I didn't have much—
nobody much had anything. But I had the little with me
what I had, and this boy carried me to his father's house.
We went in a car and we got there about dark, and when
we got there all the little kids were lookin at me and I was
lookin at them, too, cause I didn't know them and they
didn't know me, those kids. See, I never had been to the
house because it was on the other side of town and my
husband always would come down to our house, he and
Rhoda's husband. So those kids were standin around the
corner lookin and grinnin and I was scared as I could be
cause I was at the wrong place, I thought, cause I never
was away from home and I didn't feel comfortable. I didn't,
really! And so I was there, but I coulda went right back
home, and I wished I had.

But I didn't do anything after I spoke to em but just
took off to my room, sit there in a chair. I went and sit
down and I was measurin out things, how was I gonna
sleep with this man cause I hadn't been in no bed with no
man in my life. I didn't wanta go to bed. I just kept sittin
there and kept sittin there. He said, "Ain't you goin to
bed?" I says, "I ain't ready to go to bed." And so he just
kept talkin and he says, "Now remember, you my wife
now." I say, "What do that mean?" And he said, "Well,
you ain't gonna sit up all night, is you?" And I says, "No,
I'm gonna sit up till I get sleepy." You see, he knew what's
gonna happen, but I didn't. My mother didn't tell me
nothin—nobody told me nothin. So when I got married, I
had to learn on my own. Oh! But he kept talkin, so finally
I told him he better go out because I'm gonna pull off my
clothes. So he went out and I pulled on my night clothes
and I got into bed—right on the edge. So when he got

ready, he come in the bed and then he went to try to talk and play around me and—that was the worst experience I ever seen in my life. Now that's the truth! That's the way it was when I got married.

After I got married, I stayed with my mother-in-law a little while—his mother and father had a big house on a hill. She was nice in her way I guess to me, but she expected me to go and help wash all these people's clothes. You see, it was a lot of em in the family—she had fifteen children. She had fourteen living children and only one was dead. And me and her daughter Isabelle—she's in Detroit now—she and I did all that wash. They had to carry the clothes to the spring in the wagon, one of the boys, you know. They'd take us down to the spring and we'd stay down there all day long and *wash*. Oh, I never got so tired of washin. Washin on the washboard, boilin clothes in a pot, beat the clothes on the battlin block. It shouldn'ta been nobody but me and my husband for me to do, you know, and me and my husband for me to cook for. But she did all the cookin, see, and I would stay home in the mornin and I'd be helpin her gettin dinner ready. Then I'd go with those hot buckets, and I mean it'd be so *long* walkin, that sun would be so hot, carryin dinner to the field. Cause I remember me and Thompson and Henry Lee were the main dinner carriers. Thompson—I heard he's a preacher now. Howbe-ever, it was me and them and we was walk, walk, walkin and the sweat would be pourin down you. And hot. But you take the food to the field and then you worked until time to come home in the evenin. That's it.

I stayed there a few months and then we moved from there to the house that my husband was born in, and all the rest of his sisters and brothers. It was a little two-room house—it had two rooms and a kitchen. It was given to my husband from his father. So I was glad, but we didn't have nothin to take nohow. We had two beds. We had a few old chairs. I don't know where he got that old table from, but it was a made one, you know, sittin right by the window. And that's all we had—no dresser, nothin. And I brought some pots from home—my mother gave me a few. Never did add not one to it either. We didn't buy nothin.

And I had about four or five plates, and when we was married my husband gave me thirty-five dollars to go to Natchez to get me a set of dishes—that's what he was gonna give me. He gave it to me—I had done sewed it up in the mattress so I could keep it till I had a chance to go to Natchez. Then he come back and made me give him that money. I gave it to him. I never did get that set of dishes and I haven't got em yet.

But I moved to this little house and when I got there, it was holes they done burnt in the floor, and my husband had got some old stove from somebody and he got a pipe and put on the stove, and it wasn't enough to go through the roof. He just let the smoke come in the house. Oh, you don't know the half.

So we took his parents' old house, and that's where my first one was born. Benjamin, he was my oldest one, and he was born in that little house. I had three kids by my husband—there's Miles, and Jerome and Ben. Jerome and Miles was born at my mother's house. But all of em's born by a midwife—they used midwives along at the time when I was havin my babies. When you were fixin to deliver your baby they come, and they used dirt dauber tea in order to hasten labor for a woman that was pregnant. The dirt daubers always build their nests in the house in the summer because there wasn't any screens to the windows—they were board windows—so the house was open in the summer. So the nests would be up in the rafters and they'd get them and they'd put em in some water and let that water come to a boil, and they'd make tea out of it and they'd give you that to drink. You know that sound silly now! If there was anything that was doin the work, it was just the heat because I don't see what the dirt dauber was doin, do you? No. But that's the old-fashioned way that peoples had to bring labor pains, they say. So they would give you dirt dauber tea—they did it—and then they'll sit down and wait on the pains to come. And do you know the first baby that I had, I got in labor around six o'clock on Saturday and this baby wasn't born till around three-thirty on Monday mornin!

And then when you havin a baby in the country you had to stay in a dark room a whole month cause no light could come in there on the baby. Then when that baby was a month old, you took it outdoors. You take that baby and wrap it up and you go all the way around the house with that baby, and then you bring the baby back in the house. It's free to go then anywhere.

And when you'd have a baby, you'd have to wait at least a month or so before you could wash your head because they was afraid that you might take pneumonia and die. Now you can go to the hospital and take a bath and wash your head today, but you wouldn't do it when you have a baby then.

And when you menstruate—"come around," we call it—you didn't go and wash your head then either because if you wash your head at that time, say, it'll kill you. Cause one girl which was Liza Sutton, they said that she died from washin her hair when she wasn't supposed to be washin it. My father was tellin us about it. He told us girls— the three of us—but that's been a long time ago. He said, "A certain time of the month you don't wash your head." That's all he told us about that. But he should have said, "Now listen, you all, don't wash your heads when your monthly on." And then he shoulda told us, "And don't go foolin around with boys and get pregnant, and if you do, don't take turpentine and try to do away with that." But he didn't tell us that either, you know what I mean, although we didn't fool around with no boys. But I'm just showin you, this is what he shoulda said to bring it out plain to us. But he just said, "Never take turpentine—it'll kill you." But he didn't tell us for what reason don't take it. So we learned this after we got older. We learned this from Mrs. Harrison because my momma, she got pregnant too close behind me—it was an unwanted pregnancy—and so she taken turpentine and she taken too much, I guess, and she died. She bled to death and died.

And the first time I had my monthly, I was fourteen years old, and I didn't know that you were supposed to come around. But I started, and when I saw that, it really made me afraid. You know, I was afraid, but I wouldn't tell nobody. I would just hide, and I kept me a little rag, and I'd see it, I'd be scared. I was so scared. And so finally Rhoda or some of em told my mother and then she showed me how to fix myself and told me I was supposed to be like that. But now she shoulda told me in the first place. She didn't. We wasn't told things. Just like now they talk open to children, which I think is good for them to know. But they kept things hid from us—we learned it as we grew into it. That's the way we learned things.

But I had babies one after another. There's Benjamin born in thirty-one, Jerome was born two years later, and Miles was born two years after that. Then I always looked after our children such as bringin in water from an old well across the field, washin the clothes, cookin the food such as I had. And when I got the kids down, I'd go out and work till they wake up. My husband had a field in the swamp. He raised cotton and corn and sugar cane—that's what his farm was. He'd plow it, but I did the other myself. And we had a garden around the house and an early corn patch. I had a beautiful garden. I had turnips, mustard, collard greens, beets, carrots, onions, potatoes. I used to even raise my own garlic. It grows big and tall and it has little pods after it blooms, cause I used quite a bit of it in the spring makin syrup for worms—you chop it up and boil it down and make that into a syrup. That was the spring medicine for the kids to keep the worms away because they would grit their teeth at night and don't sleep well, so you give em the worm medicine. And I know when *we* were small children, my father would go out in the springtime and get hard rosin off the pine tree. He'd put it on a piece of paper and he'd take a jar and roll it out until it get real fine, and he'd put a little sugar in that powder and give it to us. He'd give it to us on the end of a spoon—just put it in our mouth and drink some water. He said that was good for worms. And then we used to take black draught. You know what black draught is? It's real nasty! It was given to us just dry in your mouth. Then you drink water behind it and it would go down. It was good for fever and colds. But the real medicine was a drop of turpentine on a teaspoon fulla castor oil would be for the little ones when they have a cold.

But I had a pretty good time not havin sick children.

And I used to get out there in the field and work a lotta days, and my husband would be plowing in the field. Then sometime he would go to town and get some cornmeal and some grits maybe and a bag of flour and a little piece of meat, and that had to last because we didn't have food that I had at home—we didn't have that. Things wasn't that good cause my husband wasn't no provider for no family. He was too lazy. He just plowed, that's all. He'd go out and plow and feed his mule. The mule was named Jake—he was iron gray. Then he'd get on his mule and go to this woman's house—come home and get the wash pan and wash a little bit here and there and get on his mule and go.

So when I was with my husband he didn't look after nothin and he'd fuss and quarrel all the time and you couldn't talk to him cause he'd cuss nearly every word anybody said. If I tried to talk to him he'd hit me so hard with his hands till I'd see stars. Slap me, and what he slap me for, I don't know. He never did accuse me of no men because I didn't have no men all the while I was married to him. I never had a boyfriend even at my home but Jamie Watts when we was comin up young. But my husband would slap me and then go off to his woman's house. That's the way life was.

Now the first time that he slapped me, I hadn't been married too long at that time, but I was pregnant then with my oldest son Benjamin. He was going to see this woman Brandy but I didn't know it. It was in the evenin that he was goin. He come out of the house and come down the steps, and when he was goin down the steps I says, "Where you goin?" And he said he was goin down the road. I said, "Well, I'm goin with you," and he said, "Help yourself."

It was in the summer and Poppa Jim and all my brother-in-laws were sittin up on the porch—it was before we moved from the big house—and they all laughin, the boys were laughin. I reckon they knew what was goin on, you know, but I didn't.

So I started walkin along with him and all of a sudden when we got down so far he said, "I think you oughta go back." I say, "Ain't you goin back?" He says, "No, I gotta go over here." I says, "I can go with you, can't I?" He said, "No, you go back." I said, "I ain't goin back." He slapped me. See, he was goin to meet this woman and he had gotten not too far from this woman's friend's house where he meets her at, but I didn't know at that time that he was meetin her there. I have passed right through this woman's yard comin from the church, and him and Brandy would be up there layin in the bed and I didn't know it until she told one of her friends, and her friend was my husband's first cousin, and she told me that Brandy and my husband was layin in this woman's bed. I'd be done went to church and that's the way I had to come home. That'd be on Sunday. But when I got slapped, I turned around and come back to the house. Didn't tell all of them about it when I got back, but that's what happened. He was somethin else! I never had it good. I never had not one happy day with my husband. Not one! Uhn, uhn. Not one happy day.

So me and my husband didn't get along because he had somebody else, too, and she was pregnant when I got married to him. But I didn't know nothin about her. I didn't know nothin about life, even, when I got married. See, when I got married to this man, I didn't know nothin about mens would go out with other women. I thought you married and that was just your husband—that's what I thought. You're raised up in the country way back in the woods— we didn't know anything. Just go to church on Sunday and back home—go to field, back home. We ate, and we played together, and we loved each other, and that's all. So I just married, cause if I hadda known anything about life, I woulda looked further.

But later on I found out that he was runnin around with this woman cause when you get married, you can hear everything. And then it came to me that she was gonna have a baby by him. She said, "Well, she might marry him, but I'm goin be an ant in her garment." You know what she mean by ants in your garment? Get in your garment and sting. Well, she was the ants all right!

When we moved back there in the woods this woman Brandy got to where she had done stopped goin to the place where she used to go for my father-in-law's house and went to comin to my husband's uncle's house. I could see it from our little house—it was nearby. When she get there, she'd sit out on the porch where my husband could see she was there and she would say, "You all gonna play cards tonight?"—loud. My husband soon get up and go on over there. He'd go on his mule to this house and they'd play cards or whatever they was doin. And the minute he start out to come home his dog would start up, "Yup, yup, yup, yup." You could tell it, you know. So, anyway, I remember one night—he didn't have money that he could give the women, but he would steal from the house and pretend that somebody been in the house and got it, like meat or syrup or something. One night he went out in the cornfield and he didn't know I was comin outside, so he had a meal sack in his overall, you know, with the apron.

He had this sack in there, and as he let his pants down, the sack fell out and I says, "What's that?" Well, he got mad with me and he just went on bolder, then, and got corn and things and take it over to this woman's house. And whenever I tried to talk to him about it, then he's ready to fight. He always fought me so till he would call me his "God damn knock box." That's what he called me.

Then one time he threw me out the window. Yes, he did! We had these board windows shut like a door—he threw me out the window because he had bought some shoes that were too small for Benjamin, the oldest one. He put the shoes on his feet and the shoes were hurting his feet. I told him, "You should take the shoes back to the store where you got em and get a larger pair," because a growin kid don't need no shoes huggin their feet. And he said, "Oh, you shut up your mouth and leave it alone. He can wear these shoes till he break them. When he get them broke they'll be all right." So he wouldn't do it and because I was askin about it, he picked me up and dropped me out the window. It was in the wintertime and the fire was in the fireplace, and as I went to reach up to get back in the house, he picked up a burning stick and he burnt me under my arm. He was very cruel to me, very cruel.

So anyway, my husband didn't do much—he just loved to run around. And I didn't have nobody to go to except Rhoda. Rhoda come and visit me every once in awhile, and I would go to visit her every once in awhile. You see, she was already married before me and she was in walkin distance to me, but it was a long walk. But I went. And I'd go home—that was a long ways but I would ride the mule home. My mother didn't come over to see me much because they didn't like my husband because they didn't like the way he treated me. They didn't like that. So I'd leave Jerome and Ben at my mother-in-law's cause I didn't take em on the mule, and I'd put the saddle on it and I'd get on the mule and ride down there. I didn't ask for the mule that often, but I would ask sometimes if I wanted to go, especially if he's in a good mood, until he made the mule bad. He made the mule bad cause he used to cuss the mule, beat on the mule, and the mule got to where he's shakin so, I didn't ride the mule no more.

But I would think about my mother and them, and then I'd see em at church on Sundays, but I didn't go to church that often because I lived on the other side of Orchard, and I had a baby on my hip if my mother-in-law wouldn't keep em. And other'n that, I didn't go no place and wasn't nothin to do. Weren't no books to read, no radios to play. We didn't have no telephone. Nothin to do but get on the bed and lay down. I'd just lay down. But I got to the place I'd rather see him gone than stay at home. I'm tellin you! I'd be glad he's gone. Oh, I've been through enough! If I hadn'ta left him, I'da been dead too long!

I left my husband and I went back two times. I separated about three times before I really made a good one cause he'd come every night—it'd be rainin or what not— he'd come down and he be beggin me to go back. The first time I separated and I went to my father's house I remember he come there and made me pull off the clothes I had on me cause he had a gun. My father said, "Give em to him," so I gave him my clothes and he carried em back home. But I went back to him that time. That was between Ben and Jerome's time.

Then once I had went to my father's house when Jerome was a baby, and he come the next night and gonna make me go home. He was gonna make me go home, and he's gonna ride the mule and carry the baby on the mule, and I'm gonna walk, I guess what he figured. I don't know. But I wouldn't go. So he's gonna take the baby and go, so he got the baby and went on. When he got over on the other side of the Buck Harrisons' home and he crossed the branch, the baby started cryin, and he knew that was a different cry and he looked, and he had the wrong baby. He had my mother's baby—he had my sister Harriet. Harriet is my mother's mother's name, so she is named after her grandmother. Harriet is one month older than Jerome, so he took her instead of Jerome. When he discovered he had the wrong baby he come steppin back. Momma say, "Oh, here he comes back. I reckon he musta thought that since you wasn't gonna follow, he'd bring the baby back cause he don't wanta be bothered." And he comes and, behold, he had Harriet and Jerome was still in bed. We hadn't missed the baby, mind you. We hadn't missed her! So he put her back and got Jerome and carried him home. I stayed on there that night. But the next day I went home.

I went home that time, but I promised if I ever left again, I wouldn't go back. So I did, and I didn't. And I'm so glad I didn't cause he was the type that liked to fight, and I didn't like to fight myself because we wasn't raised that way. I never seen my father fight my mother—I never seen him hit her in my life. Now, why would my husband wanna be knockin on me? I never did anything. If I had done somethin, it'd be different, so I don't know. But he always was mean and always fought me, and I just begin to go prayin to God—I would pray every day, "Let me get away." I wanted to get away somehow because I was gettin tired.

When I left him the last time, my brother was coming

from Bainbridge. After my brother got married, he wanted to go to work where he could make a little money, and there wasn't any at my home. There was a sawmill up there in Bainbridge, so he was workin there. But, anyway, my brother was coming home for Christmas, and when he came home somebody died—I don't remember who—but I went to the funeral, and my husband and my brother went to the funeral. So after the funeral my brother asked my husband, could I go to Lucy Randolph's? You see, my brother and his wife Rebecca was invited to their home for dinner that day, so he asked him, could I go up there? And he would bring me home later after dinner. Then we could get a chance to talk and be with each other. My husband said, "All right." So when they got through eating— see, my brother had this Ford car that my father give him what used to be our car, so he taken me as far as he could in the car cause the roads were so muddy. Then he walked the rest of the way with me. It was rainin on Christmas day.

He walked home with me, and I didn't have much oil in the lamp, so I lit the lamp with the little oil what was there. And I didn't have no fire in the house—it was cold— so my brother tried to get me a fire started before he went back. Then I hurried on and went to bed and put the kids to bed. And my husband came home—I don't know exactly when, but it was late—and he asked me, why didn't I have somethin in the lamp? Cussed. I say, "You know I got the kids." I say, "You know you the one that goes to and fro and bring in from downtown." He say, "How come you didn't get outa here and go *borrow* some?" So I said to myself, "No sense talkin to him cause you can't say!" So he asked me how come I wouldn't open my God———

mouth? I didn't say nothin, so he come to the bed and he
hit me. When he hit me I jumped outa the bed, and when
I jumped outa the bed, I just ran. And I went to the porch—
there was a porch, but the steps had been torn off, so he
had sawed a big old block, and you had to step on that
block, or if you missed the block, you fall. I missed the
block and I fell. I didn't have a gown to put on—I had on
a slip and had on a short-sleeved sweater. I left the kids
right there with him and I went all the way to his father's
house that night, barefeeted, with that on, on the twenty-
fifth day of December. That was in the dark. It was two
miles or more and it was rainin—I had mud between my
toes. Oh, one thing I really hated was that mud to come
up between my toes. But I went to his father's house and
I borrowed my sister-in-law's dress and my brother-in-law's
shoes and I went home the next day. I walked. And I didn't
go back.

My husband didn't treat me good, but where is he?
Where is he now? It's no boastin about it because he got
kilt. But I always heard that disobedient peoples don't live
the end of their life out. So, you know, he knew he was
doin wrong because he shoulda went on and married her—
she was gonna have a baby for him. And so, he did wrong,
and he didn't get to see his children grow to be grown.
But I did. Thank God!

I was in Mobile when he got killed. My husband, he
had got in with a man by the name of Mr. Steel and his
brother. Mr. Steel is a white guy. They were real mean
people. But he was supposed to have been sellin this
whiskey—shinny they call it, you know. It's white lightnin. He was sellin it for these peoples, I guess, and the
sheriff caught him with this shinny and they put him in

jail. And the sheriff told him, "If you tell us who you workin for, we'll turn you out." So he told it, and when he told it, well, the others took him one day. He had moved then from Orchard to Madison. He had an aunt livin there not far from where I was born—his aunt was named Lilly. So when he moved there with his aunt, he was workin down there, and these brothers came to this aunt's house and they asked for him. They said that the truck what they were in was bogged down and they wanted him to go and help em to get the truck outa the bog. And so, he had another brother was livin there too, T.J. T.J. say, "I'll go with you." Said, "No, he'll do. We don't need nobody but him." So right there he shoulda thought, but he didn't. I suppose he figured that they was his friends, so he went with them, and when he went with them, they just shot him and then they cut his privates out, made him eat em. I can't believe it myself, but they say that's what they did to him. That was his aunt told me this. But after they had done whatever they wanted to do to him, I know they brought him and threw him at his aunt's gate. They threw him at the gate and left him there moanin, so they put him in the hospital and he died a few days after. Nothin they could do. But he thought he was safe when he got to Madison—nobody was gonna bother him, see. But when they found out where he was stayin after the sheriff had turned them out of the jailhouse, cause the jail is in Madison, then that's the time they got him. They got him for tellin on em. Samuel, his brother Sam told me that.

But they kilt him—that was in nineteen forty-two—and I didn't care about his dyin. I didn't shed any tears and I didn't feel bad about it. Now ain't that somethin?

# FOURTEEN

◇◇◇◇◇◇◇◇◇◇◇

# *The Burden Was on Me*

I WAS with my husband about five years, and when I left my husband I didn't have nothin, so I went to Bainbridge and I lived with my brother, and my brother helped me. But I'd go to bed *every* evenin before the sun go down and cry, cry, cry before I go to sleep. Honestly! It was awful to leave my kids! The reason why it was so awful to leave em because they wasn't together. My husband peoples kept my oldest son, and my father had Jerome. This is the way it happened. When I ran out the door in the middle of the night and went to my father-in-law's house, I left the kids home with my husband. He got those kids and brought them kids the next day to his father's house, and he said that I could have Jerome and he was gonna keep Ben for himself. He kept Ben because he was the first one and he thought I wanted him, which I did. I wanted him so bad. And it just worried me because he was callin my husband's mother "Momma." That hurt me— I wanted him to know that *I* was his mother. But my father would always say, "Don't worry about him," say, "they're his grandparents just like I am. He'll be all right."

I just wanted my kids all together with me, but I couldn't stay in Orchard with them and be in peace because each time that I would separate from my husband, he would

come to my father's house and demand me go back, and I
would go back because I always figured I could make it. I
always stayed until I got another baby, and then he'd be
so mean to me, I'd have to go. So this time my father wanted
me to leave town, so I left. But I couldn't take my kids to
Bainbridge with me and take care of em when you was not
makin anything, you know what I mean? So I left town
the weekend after Christmas, and my father kept Jerome
and my husband peoples had Benjamin, so I would go to
bed early and I would cry because I didn't want to be leavin
my kids. But finally it wore off, and after it wore off, well,
I got all right.

So I went to Bainbridge and I didn't move nothin
because the only two valuable things I had at that time
was my sewing machine and my cow. The sewing machine
stayed right there at my mother's because I didn't have
nowhere to put it. It was good that I could go to Bainbridge myself because my brother had a little place. I gave
the cow to the midwife for my second son being born—
Jerome—because when he was born my husband didn't
pay the fee for the midwife. You see, my father gave me a
cow after I got married so I'd have a start in havin cows of
my own. It was a heifer cow. But it never brought forth no
calf and I didn't have no money, so I gave it to the midwife. You know, there wasn't no money in circulation then
so peoples I guess would give whatever they had like syrup
or corn to the midwife.

But I lived with my brother, and my brother was workin in a sawmill, but the sawmill wasn't payin anything,
and so I figured the best thing was to hunt me somethin
to do. I went around a few days until I found a job which
was with the Raskins. They had a hardware store, and

they knew my brother from goin to and fro, so I got the job through my brother. I was doin day's work for them. I made biscuits and cleaned house—just mop the floors and I'd dust the furniture and wash clothes, but I didn't have to wash em by hand. They had a washin machine with a wringer. The housework wasn't nothin bad to do, but look like to me I was goin there a portion of each day and I didn't get but a dollar and a half a week.

I worked for them till Mrs. Raskin's husband got ill, and then she couldn't have me any more. When I stopped workin for her I went to workin for other peoples until I went home to Orchard and gave birth to Miles. You see, I was pregnant with Miles when I separated from my husband. My mother wanted to keep Miles because he was ill—she wanted to keep him. And she didn't want me to stay home cause time I got home, here come this husband, you know, come up to my father's house, him and the mule, and he be wantin me to go back.

So then I went back to Bainbridge—I had had Miles and I didn't bring him—and I got a job workin for Dr. Chatfield. He was my brother's doctor, and that's how I found that job—through him. He lived down the road from us—it was walkin distance to go. I milked the cow mornin and night for them—I knew how to milk a cow because I had been in the country all my life, and I knew! So I'd go to the house in the mornings and milk the cow. Then I'd go to the office, and he learned me how to use a telephone and take messages that peoples called in. The first telephone that I ever had talked on was in his office. I worked there until around two o'clock, and then I would leave with those towels what he'd use and bring em home, wash em, boil em out, and dry em and press em and fold em up and take em back the next mornin. And in the evenings, I would get me a pail and come back, and I'd milk the cow again, and that milk was mine. I would carry that home for my sister-in-law to cook with and for the kids.

So I'd do that every day, and that was three dollars and fifty cent a week. I was gettin *big* money when I was workin for Dr. Chatfield! I was gettin more than usually other peoples were around there at that time because, I don't know, they seemed to have liked me. And they had one daughter named Carolyn, and I used to take care of Carolyn. They would go to Montgomery and places and leave me there with her, and they were satisfied.

I worked for the Chatfields for maybe two years. I worked for them until it was almost time for me to have my baby Vivian. Vivian wasn't my husband's child, but now Vivian is Carter Gray's daughter. Nobody did ask me nothin and I didn't tell them nothin—I didn't think it was their business. But that was my mistake right there because at that time it seemed more of a disgrace than it would be now. Nothin seems to be disgraceful now to young peoples who live with mens and they have these babies common law. But I thought it was a disgrace because I wasn't raised that way. My father raised me right, I married off right, but after that, I took on from there. But I didn't know nothin when I got married cause I wondered so much how in the world I was gonna have a baby. I was so anxious, and I found out cause I had babies one after another because I never knew how to avoid havin babies and I didn't ask nobody, so I didn't know nothin. I'm tellin you, when I got married I was just about dumb as the cat, and after I separated from my husband, I *still* didn't know nothin, so there come Vivian.

You see, when I separated from my husband, I goes to Bainbridge and I started goin around with these two girls and their friends. Let me see, how did I meet those girls? I picked cotton at these girls' field—it was two daughters and a son, and I was pickin cotton at their father's place. His name was Mr. Gray. I learned them through Miss Gussie Tillman which was a midwife—she was Vivian's midwife. I used to go up to Miss Gussie's all the time because she lived down the street a little piece from my brother, and I done worked all day and I didn't have nothin to do in the evenin but just go sit on her porch and talk. You see, she had a daughter—she was older than we were—but she would sit down and talk to us, Johnny Mae Copeland and Varnella Griffin and me. We would sit on her porch and talk and watch cars and peoples pass. That was somethin because we was livin way over in the country in Orchard and wasn't no excitement over there unlessen you saw a squirrel with wings. But one time Dr. Chatfield went somewhere and he carried Mrs. Chatfield and Carolyn and I wasn't workin at that particular time, so Miss Gussie was tellin me I could get some work with Mr. Gray cause she'd go out and pick cotton with Mr. Gray and them, too. So I went some days to pick cotton, and whatever I made, that would be money for that day. And I started goin around with his daughters and their brother was the boyfriend, so that's how I met Carter Gray.

He had a car, so I'd go around with him and his sisters and their friends. And these girls were hipped to what they were doin—they knew how to keep from havin babies—and they was carryin me along with them which I say I didn't know nothin. So I got pregnant by him, and when I got pregnant I just told him. But whenever a lady get pregnant with a man and she isn't married to him, he always go to pullin off from that one cause he gonna look for somebody else. I don't know, but that's the way they do. They will do it.

So we didn't get along after I got pregnant, so we quit—we broke up. And I didn't want that baby because I didn't have nothin to do with the man, and I didn't want my father and them to know I was gonna have another baby because I just was shamed, you know. But I was pregnant, so there was nothin I could do.

So I knew a lady named Annie—her name was Annie Williams—and she called herself a person that could do away with babies. It's my friend Johnny Mae told me about her. When she knew that I had gotten pregnant, well, she just told me, says—you know they say when you get pregnant down there you done got in trouble. "If you done got in trouble, I can tell you a good way you can get out of it." And she told me about Annie. So she suggested it, because I hadn't heard nothin about no abortion nohow. You come from the country, you don't know anything about that. Annie lived right around the corner from us. I used to go to her house and she used to come to our house, but I didn't know nothin about her business like *that*. But when Johnny Mae told me about Annie, I decided to do away with my baby, so I went around to her house and I told her cause I didn't want nobody to even know about it. And she asks me how far along and she gave me some camphor gum—you ever seen any camphor gum? Oh, that is strong! She chipped it up—camphor gum and nutmeg and I don't know what all she mixed up for me—and she give it to me and she just told me to take it. I didn't give her nothin for it, but I brought it home and took it. I took it through my mouth, and when I took it, it made me sick till every time I breathe look like heat was comin outa my nose. It made me *so* sick.

I got sick at home, so my brother went and got Dr. Chatfield and he came right away. And he wanted to know what I had taken and he wanted to know what I had taken it for. And I told him I had gotten pregnant and this lady had given me somethin so I wouldn't have the baby. So he gave me warm bakin soda water to make me vomit. If I hadn't vomited, I'da been dead. I was crawlin on the floor. So I shouldn'ta took that medicine in the first place— I should have thought about what Mrs. Harrison told me that my mother had taken turpentine because she had an unwanted pregnancy and she had died. But no, all I was thinking about was doin away with this baby. But I didn't— and so Vivian came on when the time come.

But I didn't tell my brother nothin about it cause I wasn't even showin, see? But the doctor told him. And I didn't tell my father and them anything till so long down the road Davey told em, and my father didn't say nothin to me. I hated it, but I didn't want no other baby. I couldn't hardly take care of myself, and I had other kids I'da loved to have taken care of, and I couldn't do that.

But I was gonna have this baby and I was livin at the house where my brother left me. See my brother was workin in the sawmill, but he didn't really have no *good* job. So there were some peoples that had left the sawmill and came to Cleveland, and these peoples wrote back to my brother and told him that he could probably get a job in Cleveland, too. So he went up there and he left Rebecca and the children—he had three children—he left Rebecca and the children and me in the house. And when he got up there and got him a job, he sent for Rebecca and them, and he left me in the house with the furniture. I worked for the Chatfields and I paid the little rent what had to be paid, and it was a lady stayin there with me, her name was Lucile. She knew Miss Gussie too, and a lotta time I'd see her up there. She knew that I was gonna have this baby, and so she asked me who was gonna be with me, and I told her nobody, so she suggested she stay there with me. She stayed there and when I had the baby, she fixed my meals for me and also she washed diapers and things. She stayed with me until I got on my feet.

But my mother came to Bainbridge after Vivian was born. I didn't tell her to come. Her sister's son's wife lived in Bainbridge, and she wrote her and told her that I had a little baby and needed a mother's attention and she came. She knocked on the door and I said, "Who is it?" And she say, "Hannah Brooks." And I say, "What is you doin here?" But I got up and opened the door and she said she come to see about me. Well, she was a sweet old soul and still is. So she come and she stayed about two weeks—she stayed until my father came up there after her. When my father came up there, he wanted me to go home with them. He wanted me to go home because my brother had left, but I didn't wanta go cause I didn't want my father to have to look after me like he did the rest of the kids. There was a crowd of children already there, you know. My parents had Jerome and Miles—they wanted to take them because my kids could be of some service around in the field. They could almost earn their own by workin, see? And my father treated all of em just alike. He didn't set by one son. You know, that's the way he did because, you see, I had a good father. He was very good.

But you see, my kids was my responsibility so I took care of Vivian myself, and my father and them didn't have to look after her. And I divided what I had with them by sendin whatever I could home—put a dollar or two dollars in a letter and it'd go. It wasn't often I could send anything at all cause I wasn't makin anything, but whatever I could I would send home.

So after I was married and got out I was on my own, but I wished I hadn't been out. After I had Miles I shoulda carried Miles on back to Bainbridge and I'da had somethin to keep me down instead of goin out, you see what I mean? I was doin nothin but stayin around the house and sighin all the time because I wanted the kids with me. So Varnella and them would tell me, "Child, you oughta get out and go sometime. You get out and go, you forget about your troubles." So I met up with Carter and his sisters and, okay, I went out and we went to a café way out in the country, and that's where the works took place—me and Carter and his sister and her boyfriend. And so I'm thinking he was carin for me—wasn't nothin to that cause after I got pregnant he stopped comin around. But I didn't care cause I was mad—I was mad because I was pregnant. Who wanta be pregnant for somebody that's not your husband? That's what I never wanted to be. So I was mad— you know I was! But I didn't blame nobody but myself—I could have not went with him. So after Vivian was born I didn't fool with nobody else until a long time. Oh, I didn't fool with nobody else. No! Uhn, uhn. But that's what happened, and the burden was on me.

I stayed in Bainbridge awhile and the job I had then, I was workin for some white folks by the name of Hale. He was a man that did sawmill. His wife had done had a little baby and they lived right next to us, so she just call me when she wanted me to come in and wash her dishes at night. Then I would eat my supper, and then she'd give me food to bring home to Vivian. Times were pretty hard then—I wasn't makin no money—so that was the way I got my supper. They would have rice and they'd have some kinda pork or leg bones. Whatever they had was good to me because it was better than what I had, and I was glad to wash her dishes and put her dishes away—I was. Because one time—I was taught not to steal, but this particular time I really didn't have *nothin* to eat, and when I left that day, I carried a white potato home, and that's what we had for our dinner the next day. You know, I did that once. I remember it. Now wasn't that pitiful? I didn't have *nothin*.

So I worked for Mr. Hale and I'd eat, and I was livin at the house where my brother left me in. It was a two-family, and I lived in one side, and an old lady named Granny lived on the other side with her daughter and her son-in-law. They knew me and they knew my brother and all, and peoples was nice to me because I was there and I didn't have no kinpeoples cause they had gone. So Granny kept Vivian and she didn't charge me nothin and I didn't have no money to give her cause I was just poor. But she didn't tend her nohow. I went to work one day and I came home—we didn't work that day and I had been gone about two hours—and Vivian was cryin and just wet as she could be. Granny could come right through the door, but she hadn't even been in there. I didn't feel good about it, but I wasn't payin her nothin either, so what could I do?

But when my daddy come and got my brother's furniture, I stopped Granny from lookin after her because I moved from my brother's house. I moved from there to

Slick's house. Slick knew my brother real well—my brother used to cut his hair. So I stayed there until I left, and Slick and Elnora was nice cause they didn't charge me anything either. They really didn't have nothin nice to offer me cause I was sleepin *in* the mattress 'bout as much as I was sleepin *on* it. But they did the best that they could do, you know, cause it was just a little small house. It had two bedrooms and a kitchen and a little sittin room, that's all. I had a room, me and Vivian, and they had one room. And then we used the kitchen together. So they didn't charge me nothin—I'd give em a little somethin. And when I moved to Slick's house I got another lady to keep Vivian. She was livin near me, and she stayed at home because she had a daughter named Katherine, and she kept Vivian and she didn't charge me nothin either. You see, peoples used to look after each other, but now its not that way. I reckon its because we all was poor, and I guess they put theirself in the place of the person that they was helpin. "I'm poor, and why should I charge you when you poor, too?" And I have done little things for people like help sweep the yard, and they didn't ask you to—you just would graciously do that for them because they do you a favor. So we would do things for each other and "thank you" was a big thing for a person to receive for a thing that you do for em. We didn't look for no money, you know—so it's different now.

But I was stayin with Slick and Elnora and I worked at a barrel factory in Bainbridge. I worked there until I got ready to go home. Johnny Mae was workin there and she just told me to go with her—said maybe she could get me on at this barrel factory. So I went and sho enough they hired me. I'd get up in the mornin and I'd cook me some grits if I had some, and I would have some coffee, and then I would go to work. We'd work stackin slats. The men was pullin them off a belt, and we'd be stackin em. Whether I liked the work or not, I liked the little money I got, but the work wasn't hard to me. I never did mind workin—I liked to work—but you'd have the heaviest and the hardest job all the time—coloreds. Cause we was handlin that wood and the white guy would be usin the electric saw what would be cuttin it. It was just a small little place but no white ladies were workin there—it was all colored ladies and mostly colored men. Because I know I used to work at an orange crate factory in Mobile, and there wasn't no white women workin in there either, you can believe that. And no white women were workin at the shipyard in Mobile out in the yard. White women didn't work like that—they were workin in the office at the shipyard. So I was surprised to come up to Cleveland and see how white women would get out and do a lot of their own work like white women get out and they do their yards, and I would say, "They don't do that down South." It'd be always somebody colored would be doin it. And white women doin café work and they doin custodial work and they work in plants in Cleveland. Those are the kinda things you didn't see down South cause down South at that time the colored man did that and the white man would boss him, you know. That's the way it was. We saw it. We saw it, but we didn't say nothin. At lunchtime the whistle blow, you eat your food, and then when you get through eating, why you'd be talkin 'bout your own little business between yourselves. We didn't talk about nothin else. No, we was just glad to have a job. That's the point.

Johnny Mae was at the barrel factory, and we'd go to

work together and come back together. When we'd come back from work in the evening, we'd go across the railroad track, and it was a white man named Mr. Roberts, Brady Roberts. He used to have a big peanut farm, and this farm would furnish peanuts for makin peanut butter. We used to come across his peanut field, and we could pick up peanuts because when they would take the peanuts up, would be a lot of em left on the field. So we'd take us a bag and we'd pick up peanuts one by one and take em home and we would roast them. Oh, I used to pick up more peanuts because lotta times that was my meal. Or sometime if we had a dime or a nickel, we would come by the peanut house and we'd get us a bag of peanuts. They were already shelled and roasted, and we would eat those peanuts all the way home. Many a supper I've eaten nothin but peanuts and drink water. Those peanuts have saved me on many days!

So I went to the barrel factory and I worked there for awhile, but work was bad, and I was gettin where I didn't have no clothes cause I didn't have but one nice suit—my brother bought it, sent it to me from Cleveland, and that's what I wore home. When I went home, my sister had been there, and she said when I come home, she's comin there and get me and take me to Mobile. She did, so I went to Mobile.

# FIFTEEN

## Somethin Better Gonna Come to Me

I HAD BEEN married and I had gone to Bainbridge and I come back home, and I had it in me from the time I was married to my husband that I wasn't never gonna cook for no white peoples. Now that's the truth. I said, "I ain't gonna be no white folks' cook." So when I left home and went to Bainbridge and I come back—well, I used to work for some peoples up there, but I wasn't a cook. I would make up the dough and Mrs. Raskin would make the biscuits and cook em. I didn't cook for her. But howbeever my father'd always have to take up things on credit, and the crops didn't seem to be doin so well—it was a bad year. And it was some white peoples in the town—a lady and her husband—and they wanted me to work for them. It was shortly after I came from Bainbridge. They had heard that I had been to Bainbridge—I guess he figured that I had been experiencing workin for peoples, so he told my father he would like for me to come and cook for them.

So my father told me that they was comin to interview me, but they didn't interview me because I went in the woods and hid. My father didn't know I was gonna hide, but I took one of the kids and we went in the woods like we was goin to get lightwood, and we didn't come back till they left. Essie—that's my sister—I had her with me.

She and myself is the ones would do all the devilin—we is the ones that used to kill the chickens and things. We waited until we saw the car coming way up the road, and when we saw the car up the road, we just took off to the woods, and when we took off to the woods, we just laid down and waited until they left. We wasn't that far in the woods, but we was far enough to be out of sight layin down peekin. Yes, I was layin down there peepin through the bushes.

And then when they left we just come out and we went on to the house, and when we went to the house my father say, "Where was you, Daught?" And I said, "Down in the woods," I said "cause I'm not intendin to go no place and cook for nobody." So my father said, "Well, Daught," he said, "you know, if you hadda went with them and worked down there with them," says, "that woulda helped me some." I said, "I'd rather go anywhere in the world and try to get a job and work and help you if you need help than to go cook cause I'm not gonna stay downtown and cook not no time for anybody." You see to me, cookin and livin on the place was just nothin—that's the way I felt about a cook. Because my husband had gone with a cook down there—Brandy was cookin for somebody, and my husband had a child for her. And I couldn't cook if I didn't live on the place. The place where I used to live and downtown, that was a long ways to walk to cook, wouldn'ta been? The whites lived down in town. So, okay, I wasn't gonna cook down there for none of em, and my father left it up to me. He didn't try to make me go—he just said that he wanted me to, but that was up to me.

So I wouldn't work for them, and I went to Mobile. It was in the fall that I went home, and then by springtime I left. If my husband hadn't been comin probably I would have stayed home. I woulda loved to have stayed home because I woulda been with my children. I woulda loved that. But for me, I figured I'm grown, I've been married, it's best for me now to get out and go on and get some work to do so I can look after myself and my daughter. And so I went down to Mobile. I was twenty-seven years old at that time.

My sister Sally was livin in Mobile. Her husband Bailey had done built this little house on the corner of Bell Street— that was in Maysville—so I went down there and I stayed with them until I got a job. Then when I got a job, I got me a place—you know, just a room of my own—because Bailey didn't want no kids in his house and I had Vivian with me too. Vivian was just a little toddler, you know. She was too small to go to school, and my sister wanted to look after her when I got a job, but my brother-in-law didn't want her to, so I had to get another lady to keep her durin the day. She was just the second house from Sally. So the lady was all right what looked after her, but nobody'd had too much to eat and I couldn't leave much for her, and she'd get hungry and she'd go down the street and call my sister and beg her for some food, and Sally would give her somethin to eat. Oh, it was hard. It was hard, all right. I used to worry moreso about my children than I did anything else cause I loved my children, so I did the best that I could, but it was just somethin.

But Sally and them left and come to Philadelphia. Bailey had peoples in Philadelphia, and whatever his peoples were doin, they probably told him that he could do better there. But they went, and when they went, I still stayed in Mobile. I got a room here, and I stay awhile, and I get a room there. Just from place to place, place to place. The reason why you change rooms, if you thought you'd found somethin better, you'd take that. So I'd get a room with colored peoples—it was fifty cent a week. I went to Miss Olander's and I stayed there awhile, but I didn't like stayin there because Mr. Charlie drank so much and he'd cuss, so I left that place. When I left there I went to live with Millie Hunter. Her husband was the one that wanted to go with me, and I told him to leave me alone because his wife was a friend of mine, and me and her was singin in the choir together, and I was livin there with em. So he told me if I didn't wanta go with him, I could move. So I did. So then I went to Miss Cornelia's and I stayed with Miss Cornelia until her daughter and husband came. That's when somebody stole my dress that I had put out on the line that time. If I got a chance to get some cheap material, I used to take one dress and fold it and cut out somethin by it and sew it and make me an old dress which I thought it looked all right. But you better not wash em, hang em out—somebody stole all my clothes off the line one day. I didn't have nothin left. That was in Mobile. And I had my clothes stole from me, too, when I had been in Cleveland a couple years. I made a big wash—I had done got me a used washin machine—I was comin *along* then, you know. I had washed and had clothes hangin up and I went out to get my clothes, I had nothin. I tell you!

But I moved from Miss Cornelia's and I moved in a place where I was cooking and eating and sleeping all in that same room cause I had a little gas stove what I was cooking on. I stayed there awhile—me and Vivian—but it was rainin in one corner. I didn't like that so I moved. I was movin every two, three months and every time I moved, I moved into another dump until I moved to a

house where I had one room to sleep in and a kitchen to
cook in and an outside bathroom, and I stayed there until
I got ready to come to Cleveland. But, Honey, when I was
in Mobile, I was a movin sensation! I don't think Barnum
and Bailey could move more than I did. And every time I
moved, what I had I could take it in my hands because I
didn't have nothin but a few little clothes for myself and
my daughter. So wherever I go, I got a place with a bed
and cook things, you know.

So I have moved enough, I'm tellin you! That's why I
said I want me a house someday that I can enjoy and be
free. But I wasn't makin no money, so to say that I knew
how I was really gonna get it, I didn't. But I wanted it—
you can want a thing whether you see it's gonna happen
or not.

But I'd get a room and I'd have to get different ones to
look after Vivian and I worked. When I went to Mobile, I
hadn't given no thought to what I would be doin, but at
that time when we come along, to me it seemed that we
wasn't gonna get nowhere nohow past the farm and past
workin for the white peoples because the colored women
mostly could either do fieldwork or babysit or cook and
clean house in the South. That's where I was, see, and I
didn't see that there was somethin better ahead until I got
away from it. But when I came to the North I learned that
cookin and cleanin wasn't any more my job than it was
anybody else's.

But there wasn't no good job that I coulda had in my
days come along down South, and the first work I ever
known was day's work, and my sister was doin some day's
work too. So I did day's work when I went to Mobile. I
went to work for Reverend Grant. Reverend Grant had a

wife, and I worked for them every day. I was makin about two dollars and a half a week, and I was walkin about three or four miles to get that. I remember one mornin I was goin to work—I was goin to Mrs. Grant's—and a lady called me. She says, "I haven't dressed yet, so will you go to the store and bring me some soap powder?" Say, "I'll give you somethin." I went, and I brought the soap powder back for her, and then I continued my journey. She said, "When you come back, I'll have somethin for you." I stopped by two or three times, and she never come to the door. So last one day I did catch her, she give me a bag fulla shoes, and every one of em had a hole all the way through it you could see. But she give me the shoes, and so I went on. Oh, brother! Ain't that somethin! Told me she was gonna give me somethin—to stop—and every one of em had a hole in em.

And one Saturday I went to do the work at Mrs. Grant's and then when I left, I didn't have but one dollar to buy my food with. So I came on from Mrs. Grant's, and I was gonna stop at the store. So I was walkin along and this white lady saw me, and she beckoned to me and I went to her. She was out in the yard. Said, "Will you come and help me? I want to clean up this yard and pick up these pecans." She told me she'd pay me, and I told her I'd be glad to make a little extra. So I did it. When I finished and I come back, she handed me a dollar, and I went to put it in with the other dollar. I was so glad I had two; didn't have but one. While I was out there doin that work, my dollar left. I didn't know where it went! I had it in an eyeglass case—you can open it and it'll spring back—and I had it in my purse, and my purse was in her house. So I did that work for nothin. But, you see, I coulda got at that time a nickel worth of sugar and dime worth of lard, and if you got a quarter worth of rice, you'd have a great bag of rice. But you'd nickel and dimes, like fifteen cent worth of salt pork and ten cent worth of white potatoes, and when I'd go home I'd have food. But I thought I was gonna double it this time and that woulda been better for me the next time—I could stock up on a little somethin, maybe. But she paid me with my *own* dollar! Still didn't have but one dollar, and I went on.

Those were the only two times that anyone ever did me like that, and if anybody ask me any more, I wasn't gonna have time. But I could always look over what a person do to me and say, "Well, that's okay. In a little while somethin better gonna come to me." And it has.

But Mrs. Grant, she always liked me. I never will forget, she lived on Ash Street, 1308 Ash Street. She had three children. She had a daughter—her name was Jennifer—and two sons. She was a big church worker because her husband was a preacher, so she would go to church and I would stay there with Jennifer. I would fix lunch and sometime I would—oh, I would always love sweets, so I would make her a custard and pour me a little glass, and we'd just eat that. But anyway, when they'd have church supper, Mrs. Grant would cook this gumbo, and she would have me come by the church and she'd give me gumbo to carry home. And her husband was a builder, so he had pieces of lumber out back of his garage. So in the evening when I get ready to go home she'd take me in her car, and I'd fill up the trunk with pieces of wood, and that was the wood that I kept warm with. They were good—they were real nice to me.

And Mrs. Grant was so understandable. I was workin

for Mrs. Grant when my father's place got blown away by the storm. It was in the forties, January the fourteenth, nineteen forty. And you know, I had dreamed the night of the storm that I had went home and Old Daisy got after me, my father's horse got after me and run me all night. And shortly after I waked up I heard that the storm had been through Orchard and that it had blew away my father's home. Now how did I hear about it, I can't really think. But me and Sally went home. We had to go home because we had to see what we had to do with our kids. Jerome and Miles was at my father and them's, and Sally had her baby Sonny Boy there. So we had to go home.

We went on the train and I carried Vivian cause she was little, and a cousin of my husband's brought us over to where my father and them was stayin at Mr. Randolph's house. The next day after we got there we went to the farm, and it was just amazin to see—the house that was there wasn't there any more. There wasn't anything left but a part of the kitchen floor and it was moved out of its place. No walls, no nothin around it. And you could see clothes and sheets blown away from the house and wrapped around trees so tight you couldn't hardly pull em off, and twisted up chairs and bed rails stuck in the ground. The little we had, the storm just carried it and tore it up.

And my sister's baby was in the storm too. Sonny Boy was in the storm cause Momma said she got up to give him a bottle before day and say she heard this noise and she say, "Oh, seem like it's gonna be a storm." The baby was in her arm, and when the storm hit the house it just lift up and my mother was knocked off the bed, and when she was knocked off the bed, she didn't know which way the baby went because she was knocked out. Somethin hit her. And when she come to, she was lookin for this baby and she said, "Lord, I can't find that child." And my father was running around calling "Hey? Hey? Hey?" He wanted to see how many more of the family was still alive. And they answered, "Here we are." Then he started callin for my mother, and my mother was out cross some open land, and he could hear her hollerin and cryin. He called her and he say, "Here we are over here." And she say, "I'm lookin for the baby." And he say, "I got the baby." See, the wind had blown the baby, and my father caught it by the gown. That's what they say; I wasn't there. But my mother was so glad, she come back, and they were so glad!

So they all got together and it was rainin some and the wind was blowin, and it was very dark out there because it was before day. And my father say he heard this groan and he looked and he saw Cousin Robert. He could discern things by lightnin—the lightnin flash, he could see. And Cousin Robert was on a mattress what had jammed up under a peach tree—he was layin there with his face turned up where the rain was beating in his face. Cousin Robert was my mother's sister's child's husband—my mother's sister Fanny. I never mentioned her, but that was her daughter's husband. See, after we all had left, Cousin Robert came and lived with my father as a hired person, and my father had to pay him so much for helpin him work the farm. But he was dead, Cousin Robert. His neck was broken. And my aunt Ruth got kilt in that storm— that was my daddy's sister. She was living five or six miles or more from my father, and the storm killed her and a lotta more peoples that we knew in the path of that storm.

But it was a sight to see. You could just stand there and tremble. And my mother's sewing machine got blown away and torn up in that storm. That was the second time that my father's house had been destroyed because the house burned down once before my mother died. And my father says that my mother carried me out in one arm and the sewing machine in the other. I don't remember that cause you know I was small. I don't remember that cause I don't even remember my mother. I don't even have my mother's picture because everything was destroyed. Oh, I would just love to look on a picture and say, "This is my mother." Wouldn't that be nice!

But my mother carried the sewing machine out of the house in order that it wouldn't get burned up, and then my father and my stepmother saved it for me. And when I got married, that sewing machine went to the house where I was livin with my husband, but after me and my husband separated and I went to Bainbridge, this sewing machine stayed at my stepmother's, and when the storm came along, that's when it went. And it was really sad because it was my mother's, and that woulda been the only thing that I woulda had of my mother's.

But my father and them lost everything they had in that storm, and that's the only time I ever seen my daddy cry. We had gone down to the farm and he just said, "We don't have nothin! We don't have nothin!" And he went to cryin. He cried because he was thinkin about he had the kids, he even had my children—Jerome and Miles—and he didn't have nowhere to put em and his own, you know. So he broke down and cried. He never had too much, but what he had meant a lot to him, and he said, "Everything that I had, it's gone." And he cried.

So they went to the Randolphs' house and they stayed up there until they bought a place not too far from where

Garretts was livin. They bought the place from Mr. Matthew Brown. They had some land around the house and my father farmed that. He had cane there and he had peas and some corn—easy-to-get food, you know what I mean? And he kept farming down where he was—he'd go down there on his wagon because the storm didn't bother the wagon and the mules, and no hogs got killed either. So the cotton was down there at the farm and my father would go over there, and when they picked cotton they put it in a crib, and he would stay all night in that crib with that cotton and keep anybody from stealin it.

But they been at the Browns' house probably about eight years and then they decided to sell that house. I liked that house cause it wasn't too far from the branch that I could go to fishin. But my father was ready to stop farming because he was gettin too old, so they decided to sell that house and got this other house up on the highway because they wanted a house closer to town. And a sawmill was not too far from them, anyway, so then my father sold the old farm too—he sold the place to peoples who sold the timber. He should have sold the timber off the land and *then* sold it, because it was growed up—nobody was tendin the land so it was producin pine trees fast. They just grow, you know; you don't have to set em out. But he sold his land, and I wished he hadda kept it because it'da really been worth somethin now.

But it was terrible! It was real heartbreakin for me to look on where I had been raised and wasn't nothin there—wasn't nothin there but the pear tree my father set out there behind the house. The pear tree still stayed there. I imagine that pear tree may be there now. But I never went back there because I didn't want the memory. I lived there for years because that's where I grew up, and I didn't want the memory of how everything had went.

But after that storm I didn't stay in Orchard no more than a week because Momma and them were stayin with somebody else—the Randolphs. And too I was workin. So I went back to Mobile, and I took Jerome and my brother Will, and they stayed with me. It was hard at that time, but it was so nice—I told Mrs. Grant all that had happened, and so she did all that she could to help me. She didn't pay me no more money, but she give me food to bring home, and somehow or another I made it. And when my father and them got situated in the Browns' house, Jerome and my brother went back home.

But I worked for the Grants a long time—I worked for them until my brother wrote and told me he wanted me to come to Cleveland. He say, "Why don't you come up here? You could make more here." Well, I hadn't heard anything about the North because I never known nobody to come no further than Birmingham, Alabama, and that was my sister-in-law June, my husband's sister. She lives in Detroit now, but she had come up to Birmingham to stay with her aunt, and I notice she had some nice-lookin little clothes when she come back to Orchard to visit. She had little nice dresses and brassières and things, which I didn't have. I didn't have nothin when I was with my husband. I didn't even have a brassière, and she'd lend me hers and I'd wear it to church.

But my brother wanted me to come up here to Cleveland with him, so I started to try to save up what little money I had cause when I worked in Mobile, I sent a little money home to my kids. But I saved what I could, and when my sister-in-law came down for me, I had only eighteen dollars to my name, and that was maybe a few dollars over enough to come here. If I'm not mistaken it was about a dollar and fifteen cent over. Vivian was small—she was about three—so I didn't have to pay for her on the train, so you see what the price was *then*.

So we came with Rebecca here, but I didn't have nothin to come here with but just that little money. I didn't have *nothin!* And I found this little purse—at night the train was reelin and rockin, and people was sleepin, and somebody done dropped their purse. I said, "Oh boy!" And I grabbed that purse up off the floor. I didn't know who dropped it, and I didn't ask nobody. Went on in the restroom with it—I was gonna see if it had some money in there. I was so glad—I was gonna have some money when I got to Cleveland! I think it was twenty-five cent was in that purse, so whoever it was was just like me—they didn't have nothin either. But, anyway, I'm tellin you, ain't that somethin! I've come a long ways—I've really come a long ways. I say, "Lord, I got a bed to sleep in, and it's mine, and a chair to sit on, and it's mine. I got a stove to cook on, and I got books to read, and I got a radio to play." Sometime I feel like cryin because there were so many days that I didn't have nothin. So I did progress, and I'm very thankful.

I came to Cleveland in nineteen forty, and I didn't know what I was gonna do when I got here. All I knew to do was housework, so when I come here, that was about all I could get, you know. So I did housework and the way that I'd get these jobs, they'd have these little employment offices—they were colored ladies would have em in their house. They would get these jobs, and you pay them I think fifty cent for sendin you out on a day's work. So I'd get up *early* in the mornin before day and get myself ready, and I would go with peoples in the neighborhood, cause I was surprised when I come into Cleveland, so many people livin in big old apartment houses, and all of em comin down this set of steps and that set of steps. So peoples livin around my brother, they were goin every mornin, and I would walk with different ones. We'd go clear over on Woodland—that was a long ways cause we was livin on Sixty-fifth between Quincy and Central—and we'd be at the employment office forming a line outside in order to find a job. It was snow on the ground, it was cold when you stand out in line in the mornins in order to get in so you can get somethin if they got it.

But I'd get a day and they give you a card with the name on it and the house number on it and the street, the telephone number, that's all. Then I'd go out and get the bus and go. But I didn't even know how to get around in Cleveland. I learned by gettin lost a lotta times because I worked all over, but I didn't have no dread because I had been among people after I left Orchard and went to Mobile. I mean if you was living in a place and you're not around peoples much, you kinda bashful. But I had been among peoples enough not to be that way, so I didn't think nothin about it. All I wanted was a job, and I learnt my way around myself by gettin lost, but I didn't mind askin where Central was or Scovill because I was livin between those two, so I got on either one of those buses and I made it.

But I worked for different peoples, and I wasn't makin much cause when I first came to Cleveland, I made four-fifty, four-fifty for a day's work. And one time I went on this job and the lady fooled me that she was goin pay me four dollars and fifty cent and when the day end up, I got four dollars. So I didn't like the money I made cause worked hard and got less money than I did work, but why grumble? It wasn't four-fifty for a week's work one time down South.

And some peoples try to kill you, really. One lady tried to work me to death one day. I got home, I couldn't hardly get in the bathtub. Then she called me later on, she said to me, "I wonder how do you feel?" And I says, "I'm okay." She say, "You know my husband said that I had you doin too much work today." She say, "I'm really sorry about that," she say, "but when you come back, you won't have that much to do." I say, "I'm not comin back." I didn't go back, neither. But it tickled me, when I started workin for a lady here she says, "Sara, there's a toilet in the basement." And I said, "Okay," I said, "but I got arthritis," I says, "and I ain't goin downstairs to the toilet." She says, "Oh, well, I don't mean that you just have to go down to use the toilet. I have two up here." But you see, right then you can think she don't want me to use her toilet. That was here in Cleveland four or five years ago, but I still work for her.

And when I worked for Mrs. Dodd, I used to eat in the kitchen on the sideboard and she ate in the little breakfast nook, but I didn't care—it was clean. And when I used to work for Mrs. Grant in Mobile, she would put the food on the table and I would look after it and they all would eat before I did. I never did eat at the table with them, that's for sure! To come to Cleveland, most the time you ate with them, but I knew I wasn't goin to eat at the table with the Grants cause I hadn't been eatin at the table with no white ones in the South and I knowed I wasn't gonna eat at the table with em, see? Cause Alice Garrett—that was Mr. Garrett's daughter—she would give us some cookies out the door sometime. And I know my father used to tell—it had to be a tale, but he said that one time he was travelin and he got hungry. He was round the well-to-do neighborhood—white peoples—so he thought, "I'll stop here in this place." So he stopped and he asked the lady, would she allow him to come in and eat some of that grass over there? "You can eat a little." So he's out there nibblin grass with his teeth, lookin for her to call him and give him somethin to eat. After awhile she say, "Hey, Nigger! Nigger!" He goes runnin. He thought she was gonna hand him somethin. She say, "There's a little higher grass over there." Now you look into it, you would say that she just took that person to be a fool eatin grass, and if he be fool enough to eat the grass, he deserved to eat it, don't you think?

So I know that white peoples would hand stuff out the back door to colored people that work for em, and look like to me they seemed to have thought that they were more superior than you were. But the way I looked at it, a white person might be judgin me, but I'm judgin them, too. If they seem as if they was scornful of a colored person, at the same time that they was scornful of me, I'm the same way about them. What I'm tryin to say, if my place ain't good enough for you—I ain't good enough to sit down and eat with you or I'm not good enough to drink out of a glass that you got because I'm black, I don't want to do it because this is the way I feel about me bein black. I'm black, and that's the way God made me, and I can get along just as good bein black as a person can get along bein white, although they may have a better start than I've had because when I was born, I was born poor. And some of the reason why we are poor is because we didn't have an education when we shoulda had one. Cause long time ago in slavery time they didn't want colored people to have no education. You knew that, didn't you? So the colored person didn't learn like the white person learned and so that's the way the white person got ahead of the colored, and with their better start, they are still ahead of me in the way of education or jobs.

So the biggest obstacle in my life was I had to get out on my own not knowing nothing. The reason why I say not knowing nothing, I only was a girl from the country, worked in the field, so I didn't know nothin but that. So I had to learn different in order to make a livin. So when I left home, I learnt from gettin out and goin and doin. I wasn't really book-learned, and so I had to take whatever job that I was able to handle, and that was cleanin and scrubbin floors and things like that, which—that was no disgrace cause it was somethin honest, cause I coulda been out there stealin and robbin and runnin around with men, but I didn't do that. But I couldn't have a good job so I didn't make no money so I couldn't take care of my kids like I wanted to, and I couldn't give *them* a better education either.

But I worked while I was in Cleveland for different ones, and I was treated all right because if I hadn't been, I'd have somethin to tell, but I ain't got too much to tell. But I worked about a year here, and then I decided to go back. I wanted to go back South for awhile just because I had come up on a visit and I had worked, and I had bought me some nice clothes and new shoes and a big hat, and I wanted to go show them off. I had a *big* hat—I never will forget that! Oh! I had a beautiful hat, cause I love hats anyway. So I had been singin in the choir in Mobile, so I

had to go show off at the church what I had done got a
hold to cause I didn't have anything when I left down there.
My brother begged me to stay. He said, "If you stay, I'll
rent you a place," you know, for me to stay in because I
was with his family. They had three girls, and they only
had two bedrooms, so they used their livin room as a bedroom when I stayed there because they had this foldaway
bed for the kids. But it was really too crowded for em
because I brought Vivian up with me. Edith, my niece,
and my sister-in-law Rebecca would look after Vivian when
I was workin. My brother didn't want me to pay anything,
but I'd always give Rebecca somethin anyway because times
were hard for them as well as for me. But I wanted to go
back, so I went back to Mobile.

I went back to Mobile, and I stayed there, and I worked
at the orange crate factory makin orange crate boxes. I
worked there awhile, and then I got a better job at the
shipyard. Well, in fact, the reason why I had to quit there,
some of the peoples wanted to form a union at the crate
factory, and the group voted me spokesman because
everyone else was scared to speak, and I wasn't scared to
speak up. I'd tell what I thought—if I thought it was right,
I'd speak it. And so the group put me up to do the front
talkin, and I thought that was somethin wonderful. I didn't
know I was gonna get myself fired—they didn't warn me.

John L. Lewis was down there—he was tryin to orga-
nize this union for us—so he would meet us when we come
from work in the evenin. He didn't dare to come down to
the plant, you know—he would meet us across the railroad track, and he would tell us when to meet him on
Sunday. We would meet in a lady's house—she had a big
house down near the railroad track. She was the nearest

where the biggest of the group lived, so she'd let us have a room in her house—she set up chairs for us—and we would meet on Sunday evenin.

I didn't meet at her house more than two or three times before I got fired. But this Mr. Lewis would meet with us, and we would tell him our grievous things because we needed better facilities cause we's waitin on one to come out of the toilet for another one to go in. And then it never was cleaned—didn't have nobody to clean it. Well, we was tryin to get that. And we needed better for drinkin water. Plus we wanted a little more money cause we wasn't makin anything much either. Cause I was on a machine where they peeled wood off these logs, and the wood come to you on a belt, and you'd grab it and put it through a press—a keel is what you call it. You'd run it in there and you press it down, and when it come out it'd be stretched out dry. I was *workin* on that machine—I was standing all day long at this press. And it'd be *hot* there! It was hot because those slabs that was comin through was hot. It would be so hot that some peoples fall out sometime there in that plant. And it was *noisy!* The noise was bad! So we was really workin, and we was makin about eighteen dollars a week. Eighteen dollars a week, so we wasn't gettin anything. We worked eight hours a day, and when you get ready to go to toilet, you'd have to ask somebody to take over for you, and you go. But you didn't go and stay, for sure!

So Mr. Lewis would meet with us, and he would tell us what privileges we should have and the wages we should be gettin, and he would tell us how to go about demandin what we wanted. But he wasn't allowed to go into the plant, so we'd go and take it to the head and I would tell him, "We want so and so, and we don't. . . ." I did it, and they fired me. See, it was one rotten apple in the bunch, and his name was Bolling. He was the little straw boss and, in fact, he always was Uncle Tomin man. I know you've heard of Uncle Tom—you know what that mean. Well, this man rode a bicycle, and he would meet us on Sunday as if he was in our group. He would get all the news, and then he'd take it back to the main boss and tell it. Then the main boss knows how to block what we was plannin, and I thought that was a rotten deal because he was colored just like I am, and he shoulda been tryin to help us, but he was tryin to help the boss, and the boss had money and we didn't have nothin. So he was pushin against us. He could hire and he could fire, and I think he thought I was too wide mouth cause I could talk, so he fired me.

When I got fired the group told me they was gonna help me get back on, but it wasn't far enough into the union to do no good and I had to live, so I went to try to find me another job. Some girls and I used to go over across the bay to eat. They'd say, "Let's go and get some ox tails and rice." So we'd go over there to this little café, and finally I got a job there. I bet I worked two weeks and I quit. This white lady had the café, and she had this black man that was buyin the food, and they gonna make me a cook. So this man wanted to take me one day to the store to buy some things, but instead of goin to the store, he was gonna take me to his place where he lived, and he was gonna molest me, I guess. I guess he was tryin out all the women, but he didn't try me out. Uhn, uhn. I just told him straight and plain, "No, I ain't goin there. You can go in your place; I'll wait here in the car." So he talk, talk, talkin—he made me mad. I said, "Just put me out." He carried me back to the café. I didn't go back after that—I wasn't gonna stay there with that man. I quit.

But I never did doubt myself that I could get work. I never doubted that. Wouldn't get nothin for it, but I have learned to live not above my means—I learned that. And so I never had to worry about makin a great big bill that I couldn't pay. And I didn't never worry about gettin rich cause I knew I wasn't gonna never get rich. All I would ask the good Lord for was to give me strength to work and make an honest livin and to treat other peoples right. Cause my father always told me when I was growin up, he said, "Daught, you'll never have nothin." I say, "Why?" He say, "Because you gonna give away everything you gonna get a hold of." So whatever I have, I share it with someone. To help others mean more to me than anything else. So one thing sure—I didn't bring nothin here, and when I die, I won't take nothin away. I don't care if I got rich and they took me to the cemetery, they ain't gonna be no trailer behind me carryin nothin.

But this café was across from the Alabama Shipyard, and I had learned that they might be hirin at the shipyard, so I went there and got hired and for more money. I wasn't doin shipyard work, now; I was workin in the office buildin cleanin up. I worked there awhile. Then I told this lady that hired me I was comin back to Cleveland and she told me, "Well," she say, "you go to Cleveland. If you don't get a job and you want to come back, you can come and have your job back." Her name was Lois. I liked her and she seemed to like me, but I didn't go back. I stayed in Cleveland.

# SIXTEEN

◇━◇━◇━◇━◇━◇━◇

# *I Made It*

I CAME NORTH the second time in 1944. The reason why I came back is Thomas Wood sent for me. I met Thomas Wood at the shipyard when I was workin there. They used to have these little stands where you get foods, and I went to the food stand one day, and he was there and he saw me and he spoke to me, and whatever I got that day, he paid for it, and then we'd see each other each day and talk. So that's how I met Thomas. He was a nice man—he couldn't read or either write, he couldn't do that. But he could figure in his head better'n I could with a pen, and he really could work and hold a job. So Thomas was my friend in Mobile, but he left Mobile and he and a friend of his came to Cleveland because they had learned that you can get work and a little more for it here, and that's what they were lookin at. Then after Thomas had stayed up here awhile, he got him a job at Republic Steel, and when he went to makin some money, he sent me my fare and I came here.

I came to Cleveland and I stayed with my brother a good while, but I was gonna get married to Thomas, so he got this place and I stayed there till after Eric was born. See, I got five children, I got four boys, and I got three boys that really is my husband's. But Eric is Thomas Wood's son. When I came to Cleveland I was pregnant with Eric, but I didn't know it. So when I learned I was pregnant, Thomas got this place at Mrs. Burnstein's. It was a little house over on Sixty-third Street across from the church I was goin to. And I was livin upstairs, and we didn't have nothin but two bedrooms, and her and her husband had a bedroom, and there was a little sittin room just big enough for a couch—we all sit there. And we all used the same kitchen and bathroom. Oh, I always was sharin somethin with somebody. That's the reason why I wanted a house of my own.

But Thomas came and lived at Mrs. Burnstein's a little before Eric was born, and I was tryin so hard to not let it be known that he wasn't my husband till I found out that I wasn't gonna get married to him. I was gonna get married on the q.t. and they'da been thinkin all the time that he was my husband. See, after Vivian was born I didn't have no boyfriend or no nothin, and I went to Mobile, I didn't still have no boyfriend in a long time. Vivian was nine years old when Eric came. So it goes on to show you, if I got a boyfriend, I would get pregnant. But this man seemed to be a nice man, and I watched him a long time before I said that he was gonna be my boyfriend, cause when I was workin at the shipyard, at lunchtime he would always come over to where I had my lunch, and sometime he would buy hot coffee or either he'd buy sandwiches for me, and I wanted to see whether the sandwich and the coffee was just a front or was he a good-hearted person, you know what I mean? Some men would buy you things and then they would take you out, and just because they had been doin little favors for you, they would look for you to favor them some. They would want you to go to bed with em. But look like to me he just wanted company from me because he'd come to my house some nights and we'd sit down and we'd talk, and then he would get up and he'd go. So I trusted him, and I thought this time I was gonna have a husband—I thought I was gonna get married to him, and he did too. But his oldest son told his mother, "Don't give him no divorce. If you give him a divorce, then you free him, but if you don't give him no divorce, if anything happened to him, it would be yours." See he had had a wife—they were separated—but she wouldn't give him no divorce, and quite naturally you couldn't marry a man unless you gonna be livin in bigamy, you know.

So I was intendin to get married to him, but after I saw that I wasn't I said to myself, "You goin to pay the hospital bill, not me." I was gonna see to that because I just didn't want to be let down no more is what it was, because I was let down when Vivian came. I had the whole load all by myself. Vivian's father never gave her even a straight pin because we fell out, and if he even seen her, I don't know it. He never gave Vivian nothin, but I didn't ask him for nothin. I didn't bother; I didn't care. See, I take care of my business. But I stayed there with Thomas till Eric was born, and I know he paid the hospital bill—I didn't hear nothin about it.

Then Mrs. Burnstein didn't want no baby in her house, so after Eric was born we moved to Sixty-fifth Street and we were livin with some people named Mr. Manual. Mr. Manual was a black man. Then I moved from Mr. Manual's house to an apartment in the church because, well, I had said this—that I wouldn't just go and live with a man all my life and have babies and didn't have no marriage certificate. I meant that—I wasn't goin to do it. And so after I wasn't gonna marry him I moved, and when I moved I lived in the church.

You see, I was goin to church all the time there—it was a Baptist church, Mount Dillard Baptist Church. They still got it, but I don't go there no more. But I was goin to church and there was Mrs. Adam, Mrs. Tyler, and Mrs. Stewart—those three was like the mothers of the church. And I dreamed that they come to me and told me that I'd have to give up this man Thomas if I was gonna be in the church. Look like they come to me just as plain—and so when I dreamed that, that what made me really leave him. I left him right there in Mr. Manual's house and I moved to the church, and I stayed there until I got a chance to buy the house on Lawson Street.

So when Eric was born, I went my way and Thomas went his way, but he was nice and we kept on seein each other, but not in *that* way because we wasn't gonna get married, you know. That was it. And I didn't have to file for child support because each time he got paid, which was twice a month, he would come and bring some money and give it to me for Eric. So he took care of Eric till Eric got eighteen—he did that. And, Eric, he was a kid that was always smart. On Friday evenings, Saturdays, he would go up to the stores and wave for the peoples to let him deliver their groceries in the neighborhood cause he had a wagon. He had bought him a wagon because he was a paper boy, and he had seventy-five customers every day, and on Sunday he had a hundred and some. But he would deliver those papers every mornin before goin to school, and his money that he would make, I carried him to the bank and got him a savin account. He was twelve years old then when he was doin the papers. See, we had moved to Lawson Street and I had asked the paper man to give him a route. So he got the paper route and Eric kept that paper route until he got seventeen. When he got seventeen, he had two thousand and two hundred dollars that *he* had saved. Not his father's money. When his father bring that money up there for him he say, "Momma," he say, "you take it. You use it for whatever you need it for." And he wouldn't take a dime of it. But he made his, see what I mean? He always was like that. He did me proud. And he still doin me proud.

But when I moved from Thomas to the church me and Eric looked after it—we were the custodians—so we stayed there free. I didn't have to pay no rent, so I could save my little money in order to try to get a down payment for the house I got. See, when Eric was about four years old I started back to work. Vivian was in school and the lady downstairs used to look after Eric. That was before we left from Mr. Manual's. And I would go on the West Side and work for a lady cleanin her house, but I didn't get it through no employment office. I got it through a friend. She was workin for this lady and she wanted to quit, so she turned her job over to me, so that's the way I got that job. And then another lady over there wanted me to work for her because if I am working for you, you ask me, "Do you want another day? My friend wants somebody to work for them." So it's from one employer to another one, but you see, I always was lucky to get a day because anybody that I mostly go to work for, they like for me to work for em because I always was honest. You know some peoples say you can tell if a person's honest cause if he isn't, he can't look in another person's eye. You ever heard that? He look down. But Child, I could look in anybody's eyes because that's one thing my father taught us—to be honest. The last thing I remember my father sayin when I was leavin home, he said to me, "Daught, I've always taught you to be honest." He wanted us to be honest in everything we did, and we didn't have to steal. And he said, "Whatever you do, do the best that you can at all times. And if a job is just begun, never leave it until it's done. Be the labor great or small, do it well or not at all." Now that's what my father told me when I was leavin home after I had separated from my husband, goin to Bainbridge where my brother was. That was his motto, and so I always never let that left me.

So I was doin housework in order to save my little money because it was gettin deeper and deeper in my mind to "Get your own. Get your own. Get your own." I wanted my own home because when I was at home in Orchard, we had our own place to live. When I got married and moved into that little shack, it was our own place. And when I moved from there I was just in every little hole and corner tryin to live—tryin to make it. And I used to work five days a week and course I didn't never go nowhere cause I didn't have but just a few friends that I liked to be with. I didn't like to be with the girls that was loud-talkin, drinkin, and all that. You know, some girls talk loud to attract others. I didn't like that kind. And I didn't like peoples that drink because I didn't drink. So I had a very few friends that was about like me, and we would get together at each other's house some evenings, but we didn't have nowhere special to go but to church. That was the biggest outing I'd have—I'd go to church every Sunday. And I spent a lotta my time readin true-story books—I used to buy em all the time and just read. So I just woulda loved to have had a nice decent place to live because I'm to myself. I like home—I love home. But when you don't make nothin, you can't expect to have nothin, so that's the way it was.

But I always wanted a better place to live and I had got tired of movin, but you had to move because it's always move or pay more. So I figured if I once get me a house of my own and get myself settled in it, I could live in peace. And, too, I had my kids—they had come to me—and I wanted a place for them.

The first one to come was Jerome. My brother was at home—Will—he went to Philadelphia to stay with his sisters up there, so Jerome wanted to know why could Will go to Philadelphia and stay with his sisters when he was there workin in the field, plowin the mule, and wanted to come up where his mother was. My father say, "Well, if you want to go stay with your mother, you can." You see Jerome is the one that they kicked. When my husband fooled around with that Mr. Steel and his brother and got killed, then the white peoples in Orchard started pickin on my son Jerome. What happened is, he was downtown and he was just walkin along, and so a white man passed by and kicked him in his behind and told him, say, "Get outa the way, nigger!" and kicked him, you know. And so Jerome went home and told my daddy, so my daddy say, "Well," says, "begin to get picked on a little bit." Jerome say, "Ain't gonna pick on me like they picked on my father." So my father thought it would be good for him to leave from down there because he wasn't gonna take too much, Jerome wasn't. He won't bother you if you don't bother him, but don't bother him. So Jerome came here when he was fifteen and he lived there at the church with

me—Vivian and Eric and me. I had two bedrooms there
and a kitchen and a livin room. I liked it. But Jerome stayed
there at the church until he got married—all my kids are
married—and he works at a plant that makes car parts for
Chrysler.

Well, okay, Jerome was the first to come. Then Miles
had to come because my father didn't wanna keep him
down there no more because he wouldn't mind him, you
know. So he wanted me to come and get Miles, so I went
down there after him. And I hadn't seen my parents in
about seven years, and I hated so bad when I stayed off
that long time and went back, my father had got white-
headed. They were still in the Browns' house, and they
were doin okay, and they were so glad to see me. Everybody come by, my father said, "Daught's home. Why don't
you stop in and see Daught?" And we had good food to
eat, and he was askin me about Cleveland because he never
had been no further than Selma, Alabama, because it would
be just work and pay up and work and pay up and keep
the family goin is about all he could do, you know. So I
told him about bein in the city and ridin the streetcars and
goin downtown. And so when my father and them came
here to visit me, first thing I took them downtown to the
five-and-dime where you could eat at the counter. They
used to come to Cleveland about once a year—they started
comin here before I got the house on Lawson.

So I enjoyed every bit of the time I was home. But I
was shamed because I had stayed away so long. I was
writing to my parents to let them know that I still loved
them, and I was sendin money home to help them because,
you know, they raised my kids, and it was good like that.
So we kept good communication between us, but I was so

busy workin and nobody was goin there, so I didn't go back until I went after Miles. Then after that visit, whenever somebody was goin, I'd go. I went there about three times with my brother. My son Miles carried me when he got big enough where he owned a car—he carried me one time. I went down with my cousin T.J. and his wife—they carried me once. And then a year before my daddy died I went with Jerome.

My daddy died in January, nineteen seventy-eight. I was up here working, and I was asleep because it was night, and the phone rang, and when the phone rang it was my mother on the other end. "Daught," she said to me, "I want you to come home," say, "your daddy's sick." I say, "Momma, I'm leavin tomorrow." So I called my son Ben and I told him about my daddy bein sick and he says, "Each one of us give you fifty dollars apiece so you can be on your way." So my sons each gave me fifty dollars. And I called Rhoda and told Rhoda about it and she say, "I'm goin too." Rhoda come up about ten years ago so she could stay with her son. So me and Rhoda caught the bus the next day and we went. When we got there my father was in bed, so I sit down and we talked and we talked. And I remember he looked at his hands and he said, "These old hands have worked *hard*." He said, "I have worked *real* hard. And I done the best that I could do." And that's the way he always was—he did the best that he could do. And I appreciate it, and I look back and just thank God.

I stayed two weeks and then I left and came back because I had to do my work to keep goin. So when I got ready to go, I kissed him and I left. And I was here a week, and then he died. My mother got him up that mornin and he ate, and then he looked at her and said, "Well, I'm gonna leave you this mornin." Say he just grabbed her hand and he's gone. So that's the way he left. He was ninety-four. Oh, I miss that man. I oftentime think about him. I do.

And Momma's still down there—I call her once a month and she comes here once a year. I'm always glad to see her, but I haven't been down there since my father died. I've never been home when my father wasn't there sittin on the porch, and I don't want to go now and he's not there. It's just like breakin the ice to do somethin that you never did before—that's the point. So I hate to go there now—I just can't. And, too, I got all my kids here, and I have a home, so that's something to stay here for.

But I went down there and I brought Miles back here. He was about fifteen because that was about two years past when Jerome come, and they two years apart, a little better. But Miles had been ruling my father around and my father had got tired of him so that's why he give him to me. But what he did because he couldn't rule me, he hops up and joins the army. Now Miles is a security guard— that's what he is.

Then Benjamin was the last one to come. Jerome wanted his brother to come, but Benjamin didn't wanta come cause he's afraid on accounta his grandmother. Cause one time I went up to my husband's parents' house to get him and I was gonna take him with me back to Mobile and Ben wouldn't go. He just whooped and he hollered and he cried. And I asked him, "You don't wanta go?" "No, cause my grandma say if you ever come up here and I leave here with you, she's gonna put the police at me." And she believed in voodoo, and some woman livin on the hill there, she would tell Ben, "If you leave here, I'm gonna have Mrs. Collier bring you back here, and you ain't gonna be

able to walk." Oh, she had him afraid to go with me. Now
I'm his mother!

So one time I went back to see him—you know, I always
went to see my kids when I lived in Mobile. Not a lot. I
couldn't because I was workin, but I wasn't makin that
much, so I didn't have no money to be goin all the time.
But I made it home more than once a year, and sometime
I'd go home for the revival. You see, I always knowed
Momma's gonna have that trunk fulla food. But I'd come
home to see my kids and I went one time and I didn't
never get to see Benjamin. So the next time I said, "This
one night I'm gonna stay over at my father-in-law's house;
I'm goin to see him." So I went there—I carried Ben some
clothes. I bought him some sandals for his feet, pair of
pants, a shirt, and some socks. And I got there and I asked
em, I says, "Where's Benjamin?" "Well, he's out. Didn't
never come home yet." They didn't do nothin but work
the poor child to death, you know. And I imagine she would
hide him out just to keep me from seein him when I go.
So I told em, "Well," I say, "maybe I'll see him cause I'm
spendin the night tonight." Child, when I went to bed,
you know he still hadn't come home! I didn't go to sleep.
I stayed in the room—the first night I married I was in that
room. But my husband wasn't stayin there—he was stayin
in Madison with his aunt at that time. So I got up way over
in the night and I tipped out of the room and I went to the
kitchen—there was about five kids plus my son Benjamin
layin crossways on the bed. They couldn't lay lengthways
and have room, so the little kids were layin crossways,
and all of em overall pants was rolled up to the knee which
they had worked in. That's the way they were. And I looked
at him and I went over and kissed him—he ain't never

knowed I kissed him—and I went on back in my room. She got the kids up *early* that mornin, out they go to the field. But I saw him—and their little feet would be hangin over the side of the bed.

At that time Benjamin was about seven or eight years old, and as time went by, I worried about him. I worried about him, and I almost cried when Rhoda told me about Benjamin was so little and he would be out in the field plowing, you know, the mule, and he be singing about "a mother's child have a hard time when the mother's gone." See Rhoda didn't live too far from the field, and she say that what he'd be singin cause he always loved to sing and you could hear the voice in the country I don't know how far. So he was over there singin and Rhoda heard him, and she told me about it and it almost made me cry to hear it. But I couldn't get him to leave because he was afraid of his grandmother.

But Jerome went and got him one day because Jerome always was the one that he know how to do things. It was a friend of his, we called him Buddy Watts—that's Jamie Watts' cousin. He lived up here—he still do—and he had a car, so he and Jerome went and got him, put him in the car, and they brought him here. He had got to be nineteen he come, he didn't have nothin but what he had on. And he didn't want to leave then, but they kept on bringin him, and so he got here and now you can't get him back cause he's doin fine. Benjamin is a landscaper. He works for himself.

So I come up to Cleveland with Vivian, and after I came up, the rest of my kids came up here. I was glad—I was *very* glad because I had wanted em with me all the time, but I just wasn't able to support em, and then I didn't have no place for them, either, when I left and came to Cleveland cause I came here to my brother's. But after I got away from my husband and from Mobile, Alabama, and got here in Cleveland, I started to progressin and then my kids came. When Miles came I was still livin in the church, and I went to workin hard then and every dime that I could save, I would put it in my savin account in order to try to get a down payment for a house. And people would come to the church and instead of bringin their dinner if they wanted to stay, they would come and eat with us. So one day Eric say, "Momma," say, "we ain't never gonna get outa this church if you don't stop feedin peoples." A lady heard it and I reckon she musta told the rest of em because they did stop comin around. So then we stayed there awhile longer until I found a house through the real estate office. And I was lackin two hundred dollars of havin seventeen hundred dollars to pay down on the house, so my brother lent it to me because he always looked to helpin Girlie. Oh, boy! He was the *best* person. He sure was nice! He was nice to everybody because that was his make-up. But I asked him to loan me the money, and he lent it, and when I tried to repay him, he wanted to let me keep it, but I said, "No, I'll give it back to you." And I gave it to him. But when the papers came through, I moved. And I was the only single lady livin in the church, and I was movin out and they wasn't movin out. And I'm sure they laughed at me sayin, "She is a woman ain't got no husband and buyin a home. Just watch her lose it!" I didn't hear nobody say it, but I can just imagine in my heart that they were sayin that. But I was determined to get out because I'm determined to do what you tell me I ain't.

So I moved to Lawson in fifty-seven. My brother had

already bought him a house on Henderson and that was
about three streets over from Lawson, so I found a house
that was near him, and that was good. It was a big house—
I had four bedrooms, I had a den, I had a living room,
dining room, and kitchen downstairs. In the kitchen was
a window seat and house flowers. And two finished rooms
on the third floor and one bathroom and a lavatory. It was
really nice. I kept my place clean and our yard was like a
carpet, Eric kept it edged up so pretty. And what make it
so cool, it was comin up to Mother's Day, Eric went and
bought five shrubs and he set them around the porch. And
the flowers we had—I had jonquils and I had brown-eyed
Susans and I had rose bushes. So Eric helped me, and peoples passin would stop and look and say, "This is the nicest
home and yard on this street." But it was pretty.

I lived on Lawson seventeen years, and then when Eric
got married I sold that house and I came here to this little
house. But I was so glad to have my own place! I loved it!
And I never one time got a past due notice from either one
of the houses that I was buyin. But the first house I had to
have roomers because at that time when I moved there on
Lawson I had to buy a new furnace. I didn't know I was
gonna have to buy one, but I got the furnace on time, so
that's when I started havin roomers. And when Vivian got
married, I let her and her husband stay there, and he was
workin and he paid me for them stayin there.

So I paid for the house by havin roomers and workin
every day myself. Plus I cleaned the church cause when I
left the church, I still had that job. Some women woulda
had a man to come and live in the house and had an outside boyfriend, too, in order to get the house paid for and

the bills. They meet a man and if he promises em four or five dollars to go to bed, they'd grab it. That's called sellin your own body, and I wasn't raised like that. I didn't do it. No, I didn't. It has been hard for me—me bein a woman, no husband—but I'd rather do without because my grand-mother used to tell us, "If you fall, don't wallow." So if I was down now, I'd hold my head higher, just higher—that's the way I would do—because I had a hope ahead that I was gonna do better. And I tried in all my life to do things that were decent, and the reason why I had two extra kids because I didn't know nothin. It was not a happy thing because I would rather for them to have come in my marriage. But they didn't. But Rebecca always say that those were two God-sent children because I didn't have no daughter and then Eric is so good to me. So they're here and I wouldn't take nothin for neither one of them. But after Eric came along, I didn't have no boyfriend. I didn't want one because what I wanted, I worked for it, and that was that home.

So I paid that mortgage because I worked. I was doin day's work cause I didn't really have no skill, you know, cause I quit goin to school when I got married. My father didn't encourage me to marry cause, you see, older peo-ples can see further than you, so I guess he saw that the man I was gonna get married to wasn't gonna be worth bein married to. He wanted me to finish school—he wanted me to go to college—and I wish I had because I did have a little exposure of workin in the doctor's office in Bain-bridge, so if I hadda just thought and come on here and started to goin to school and taken up nursin, I would have been a nurse. But I never asked—I didn't try. After so long a time I went to thinkin back that I should have done that, but it's past the time, then.

But if I could live my life over again, I would try and do somethin for somebody else, like there is so many kids that don't have parents to really care for em. It's just a whole lotta kids that could really be corrected now if they had somebody would spend the time, don't you think so? I do believe that! And that would be one field I would love to be in.

If I hadda known like I know now, though, probably I mighta been a movie actor. But I hadn't never heard of it cause we had a victrola, you know, with the dog sittin at the end of the horn—it was in the company room. And we'd have records—we'd buy records and play records. You wind it up and play the blues—was Bessie Smith and Louis Armstrong. Was he in circulation then? I know we had Bessie Smith. But to have a radio to bring in the news, and a newspaper, we didn't have it. So I didn't know anything about movie stars—I didn't know Cicely Tyson then, you know. I really like the way she acts her parts. She is *good!* And I believe I coulda done just as well if I hadda had the opportunity. You'd have to have somebody ahead of you that know more than you to keep pullin you on, right? Not knowin nothin, born in the country, raised right in the country, I couldn't just walk right out and be an actor. But I would have been a good actor if I hadda had the opportunity because I haven't got a chance to act what I had in me.

But one thing I really am glad that my mother and my father taught us how to work. If they hadda let us been shackin around and not workin, we wouldn't be what we are today. We'd be somewhere still tryin to live without workin and makin an honest livin. But they taught us to *work,* and we worked, and that's somethin I really appreciate, and I always will. My kids work, too, and I hope they'll teach their children to work cause that means a *whole lot.*

So I worked, and as the jobs went to opening up more and you gettin more for what you did, then that's the time that I started progressin. And I can sit down in peace because I can cook without going and gettin wood, and I can go into my room and turn on my light. I can go to faucet and get me some water and get in the tub and take a bath. None of these things I had cause I have lived in places—out in the yard was a pump, and you'd go out in the yard, you'd get this water, and you had to heat the water in a wash basin and wash up. You didn't take a bath cause you didn't have no way to take no bath. And peoples used to have chambers. Well, I didn't have no chamber, so you know about what I used! Get up early and take to the "big toilet." That's somethin you never known of. I know what I'm talkin about—I've had a time!

So it may not have worked out like I wanted it—my husband didn't turn out, and then my kids was divided up. But I looked up and not back and just kept on tryin, and now everybody's together here and I own my own home. And do I give myself credit? No. You know who I give the credit to? The Lord. You know why? He gave me the strength and he give me the mind to go on. That's why I made it, because a man is not able to direct his own step. So thank goodness I'm able to thank the Lord that He brought me through all this up until now. But since I was here in Cleveland, I have dreamed about the peach trees out there in that field between the garden and the house. I saw all those peach trees, and they were hanging just so fulla fruit. They were so pretty, and I don't know why, but I didn't get a chance to get any of it.